Food for Life

THE SPIRITUALITY AND ETHICS OF EATING

L. SHANNON JUNG

FORTRESS PRESS / MINNEAPOLIS

Scripture quotations are from the New Revised Standard Version Bible, copyright © 1989 by the Division of Christian Education of the National Council of the Churches of Christ in the USA and used by permission.

Cover art: *Still Life with Fish & Asparagus*, Erik Slutsky. 1999. Oil on canvas. © *Erik Slutsky/SuperStock.*
Cover and book design: Zan Ceeley

Library of Congress Cataloging-in-Publication Data
Jung, L. Shannon (Loyle Shannon)
Food for life : the spirituality and ethics of eating / by L. Shannon Jung.
        p. cm.
Includes bibliographical references and index.
        ISBN 0-8006-3642-2 (pbk. : alk. paper)
        1. Food—Religious aspects—Christianity. 2. Dinners and dining—Religious aspects—Christianity. I. Title.
BR115.N87J86 2004
241'.68—dc22
                                                          2004008043

The paper used in this publication meets the minimum requirements of American National Standard for Information Sciences — Permanence of Paper for Printed Library Materials, ANSI Z329.48-1984.

Manufactured in the U.S.A.
08   07   06   05   04   1   2   3   4   5   6   7   8   9   10

FOR
Michael
Heidi
Rob
Nate

children
table companions
friends

Contents

PART TWO
EATING AND FOOD SYSTEM DISORDERS

PART THREE
EATING FOR LIFE

CONTENTS

Preface

Centuries of secularism have failed to transform eating into something strictly utilitarian. Food is still treated with reverence. A meal is still a rite—the last "natural sacrament" of family and friendship.
> —Alexander Schmemann

One cannot think well, love well, sleep well, if one has not dined well.
> —Virginia Woolf, *A Room of One's Own*

Eating and the Goodness of God

THIS BOOK WILL HELP PEOPLE learn to enjoy their lives more—perhaps much more. Recognizing the goodness of God in our eating is one way to discover such delight and joy.

Unfortunately, those of us in the United States and other affluent nations have inherited a worldview that diminishes our joy. This view sees life as a business to be managed or as difficulties to be overcome rather than a gift to be enjoyed. Such a view says that we can produce joy by just going out to buy something. Yet, emerging research points out that people who are wealthier are not necessarily happier and that fulfilling all of one's wants does not automatically usher in enjoyment.[1] Other research suggests a basic level of economic and material sufficiency is conducive to greater happiness than an insufficiency.

In contrast, we have all encountered people who have nothing by material standards or who have serious problems, but who nevertheless enjoy their lives. Some of them share their joy with others. They share despite their poverty. Yet those who have much often have trouble sharing and enjoying. Does the capacity to share spring from the capacity to enjoy?

Besides increasing our joy and our ability to share, this book can help us attack the problems of hunger and maldistribution of food in the world—first, because God wants us to, and second, because we cannot be profoundly joyful unless we do. Our complicity in and fear of the problems of hunger often jeopardize our capacity to enjoy.

The dominant cultural worldview suggests that scarcity lurks just beyond the present moment. We feel we must work all the time, and competitively, to avoid scarcity in our own lives. We wrest a living from the soil or the spreadsheets or the classroom or the hospital or wherever. Life becomes the business of working hard to avoid unhappiness. Of course, we also spend a great amount of time just avoiding calamity. Clearly, some sources of fear are very real. For example, our government in the United States is spending billions of dollars to ensure homeland security—or the perception of security. The price of being ever vigilant, however, often comes at the cost of enjoying ourselves. In short, when we live a controlled and managed life, we worry about every aspect of life and fail to enjoy it.

The alternative view is that we are created to enjoy life. For me, this includes eating and biking. What do you enjoy doing? Much of what we enjoy is not under our control but arises from sources beyond us. Sometimes we just enjoy whatever life brings us—we enjoy just being, hanging out, living in the present moment. Enjoyment is mysterious. We cannot produce it; we simply have to appreciate it. Rather than seeing joy principally as something for ourselves, this alternative view suggests that we can contribute not just to our own but also to others' delight. All of us are connected to each other and to life in such a way that our enjoyment reinforces and increases that of others, and others' enjoyment increases ours. Thus, we all have a stake in others' and our own enjoyment. We are an ecosystem.

The messages we get about food are among the most transparent examples of these contrasting worldviews. Eating is something we do every day. We can approach it as a task—something to produce or consume—or we can approach it as something to be experienced, an occasion for appreciation and enjoyment. Richard M. Fewkes, a Unitarian minister, says, "Nothing so basic, so central to living as food is without religious, moral, and psychological significance. We can learn much about ourselves from what we eat, how we eat, and when and where and why and with whom we eat."[2]

Clearly the church has a stake in the clash of worldviews. Sometimes the church has tended to see life as a task to be completed rather than an occasion for grace and enjoyment. Sometimes the church shares my view that the world is a place where God's grace is active in many ways, including in and through all people. Which message will the church proclaim?

THIS WHOLE BOOK IS ABOUT EATING and living to the glory of God, delighting and sharing. There are four basic steps to the argument. The first step (chapter 1) explores our desire—our hunger—for complete nourishment. We hunger for food and drink but also for fulfilling purpose in life and for acceptance. Our hungers or desires are clues to our needs.

The second step of the argument—chapters 2 and 3—examines God's purposes for eating. Chapter 2 scans the Bible to discover those purposes and to help us discern which experiences come from God and which do not. Christians affirm that God is present in human experience here and now just as God has been throughout history. This chapter locates God's presence in two basic human experiences: delight and sharing.

Chapter 3 turns to theological tradition, the wisdom of the church over the ages, to explore God's purposes for eating. Built on the biblical foundation of chapter 2, this chapter offers a theological interpretation of the contemporary meaning of the experience of eating. Some of the central theological beliefs and practices of the church involve eating, including the practice of saying grace and the sacrament of Eucharist (the Lord's Supper), as well as fasting, feasting, abstaining from meat on Fridays, and avoiding gluttony.

At this point we will have formulated a Christian ideal for food and eating and can explore how our eating patterns fail to reach the ideal. Chapters 4 and 5 turn to eating disorders to indicate the patterns of sin that characterize our eating, as well as to locate the sources of these disorders. The fourth chapter approaches eating disorders in our personal and interpersonal lives—including not only bulimia and anorexia but also overeating, undereating, or compulsive eating. Can spiritual disciplines help overcome eating disorders? How does God relate to people with eating disorders?

Chapter 5 considers the disorders evident in our global food system, focusing on the environmental and social costs created by the current structure and economics of that system. Who pays for the food we eat: what parts of the environment, what sectors of society, and which peoples? Perhaps the most economically neglected people are farmers and rural communities around the world that are pressed to produce food as cheaply as possible. What are the costs of a global system under such pressure? By identifying the reality of human sinfulness and tragedy in the food supply system and in our eating patterns, we in the affluent North are implicated in the global food disorder because such injustices benefit us. The concluding sections of chapter 5 describe our complicity and its effects.

The fourth and final step of our argument sets forth ways of recovering God's order for the world's food system. Chapter 6 asks how we can reverse the disorders described above. How can we discover God's redemption? This chapter suggests ways of coming to awareness and acknowledging our own complicity in the system. It suggests that we can confess those sins and receive pardon for them. The bulk of the chapter is devoted to the third step—repentance and transformation.

In chapter 7 the focus broadens to give more corporate and institutional scope to the work of redemption of the food supply system in the church. How can we say grace in church? Though the church is more or less visible throughout this book, here we consider the indispensability of the church for Christian solutions to personal and global disorders. We look at the ways the church can move toward reversing food disorder in its own life and in its public ministry. We explore how, through God's grace, the church can restrain evil and work for an equitable worldwide system in which all can enjoy sufficient food and material necessities.

Only then can we truly delight and share. Then our enjoyment will indeed be whole as we say grace with a full heart and open hands.

Acknowledgments

The number of people who have contributed to this book staggers me. It seems that everyone has opinions and preferences about eating! The most astounding thing has been that virtually everyone with whom I talked about this project had a food story. Many of these conversation partners have impacted this work in unseen ways.

Among those whose influence was formative are the Rome Center of Loyola University of Chicago and its environs, where my family spent a happy sabbatical, and especially Alda and Luigi de la Penna, who did so much to convey the joy and beauty of Italian life and eating. The University of Dubuque and Wartburg Theological seminaries have been my professional home and blessed me with leisure to write and colleagues to think with. Virtually all the faculty members have critiqued some portion of this manuscript; Craig Nessan has been an especially valuable colleague. Other groups have heard and responded to portions of this project: The Wabash Center Workshop for Theological Educators in Rural Ministry; the Western National Leadership Training School of the Presbyterian Church (USA); various PCUSA presbyteries; and Evangelical Lutheran Church in America synods. I have been enormously enriched by my association with farmers, small business owners, church members, and pastors in the town and country churches and communities where most of our food in this country is grown. Thanks are due as well to Liz Goodfellow at the Center for Theology and Land, who has made the work of the Center produce a higher yield.

I want to express a huge debt of gratitude to Ted Gifford, MD, who loves to talk about bodies, and an even larger debt to Patricia Beattie Jung who shares with me even more than her theological agility and thousands of great meals. I dedicate this book to my children, with whom I have shared table and kitchen for twenty-eight years: Michael, Robert, Nathan, and Heidi.

Students in my Theology of Eating class really connected with this project. My thanks to those who critiqued the whole manuscript: Margaret Snyder, Bo McGuffey, Sylvia Kirby, and Linzy Collins. To all those students who pushed and prodded, it was fun!

The folks at Fortress Press have been wonderful. Thanks to Michael West for his enthusiasm and verve; to Zan Ceeley for her design instincts; to Bob Todd for his cooperative spirit; and to Leeann D. Culbreath, whose copyediting was too often just right.

Finally, I express my anticipated debt to those who read this book. I'd love to hear your comments: sjung@dbq.edu.

Peace and joy!

Part One

God's Purposes
for Eating

Hungry for More

In this condition, we have many commodities but little satisfaction, little sense of the sufficiency of anything. The scarcity of satisfaction makes of our many commodities an infinite series of commodities, the new commodities invariably promising greater satisfaction than the older ones. In fact, the industrial economy's most marketed commodity is satisfaction, and this commodity, which is repeatedly promised, bought, and paid for, is never delivered.

—Wendell Berry

As we learn how to glorify God in our bodies (1 Cor. 6:20), we can see how our physical desires are not just needs to be met, but opportunities to encounter God's goodness, serving God's love here and now.

—Robert Morris

A Cornucopia of Food Experiences

PEOPLE WERE WAKING UP in Amalfi, Italy.

The little town, nestled in a coastal valley, was bustling on Saturday morning. The entire population of school kids was climbing up the hill (yes, school on Saturday!), and the fruit and vegetable vendors were setting up.

The vendors had driven in early; who knows how early they had to get up? They were unloading crates of the most delectable fruit—

giant Sicilian blood oranges, reddish inside and sweet; pears so juicy they almost burst; apples of six or seven types. And the vegetables—onions of all colors; tomatoes still bound together by their vines; chicory; artichokes; cabbages whose leaves looked like variegated road maps. This was truly an abundance of food.

The older women and men (mostly women) who came to shop early were there before the trucks were unloaded. They clearly knew the farmers' schedules and anticipated them. "What's good today?" "How wonderful those look!" "What are you charging for the onions?" By 8:00 a.m. there was already a procession of shoppers up and down the hill laden with bags full of the best of everything. I flashed back to the wonderful farmers' market in the shadow of the state capitol high on the hill in Madison, Wisconsin. As in Amalfi, Saturday was a special day for food.

Our friends and guides for our weekend excursion in Amalfi, Ken and Stephen, know food: international and domestic. My wife and I have eaten so well, and so often, with them. Without Ken and Stephen, the food would not have been flavored with such good conversation. On this Saturday—clear, bright, and warm—the beauty of the mountains sheltering our hillside rental pushed us down toward the Mediterranean. We took a long hike later that morning up into the mountains, past Roman ruins and waterfalls and lemon groves.

The town of Amalfi differed from our neighborhood in Rome, Italy, mostly in its topography. But we had our favorite fruit and vegetable vendors there as well: the married couple who love to carp at each other and an older gentleman, shy around foreigners. We too lugged groceries up the hill. We learned what it cost to buy too much milk or fruit juice or wine. By the end of the trip home, carrying too much weight cut into one's fingers. We came to appreciate food in a new way. We got closer to our food, ate closer to the vine and to the pasta-maker, and were more cognizant of what it took to move from field to table.

We got hooked on our local *alimentari,* or grocery store. The butcher, baker, stocker, checkout women, and boss were all related to each other. Most days the family quarrels were confined to the back room; occasionally they spilled out into the public area. The whole family, to varying degrees, put up with our stumbling Italian and even instructed us about the food when the store wasn't too busy. I loved it. I even felt guilty when we shopped at the SMA, the supermarket down in the piazza, instead of *Fratelli Ugaldi's*.

Sadly, it's when we're caught up in glorious abundance that we are often blinded to others' very different food experiences. That little mom-and-pop store reminded me of shopping at Mister David's store back in Zachary, Louisiana, when I was growing up. My world of experience in Zachary as well as in Rome was idyllic. There were hungry people in both places, of course, but the social structure of my white, middle-class world segregated me from the hungry, the poor, and African Americans, to say nothing of people of other races. Somehow, it was thought, the recognition of poverty or racism would shatter the idyll. To be sure, we saw beggars in Rome, in the metro stops, along busy streets in central Rome. The opening sign of their placards always read, *"Ho fame"* ("I am hungry"). Often they would have little children with them going from person to person, collecting donations with, invariably, a fast-food drink cup. But what was amazing to me was how carefully, how invisibly, the hungry were separated from my daily life.

In Monte Mario, the subdivision where we lived in Rome, there was no begging and there were no "gypsies." "Gypsies," in fact, is a term that is used often to denigrate, to exclude, and to discount all poor people as peripatetic, lazy, and immoral. The derogatory stereotype is used to justify and whitewash the "respectable" world's complicity in the hunger and poverty of the poor.

We found ourselves amid a cornucopia of food experiences in Italy. The wonderful, the idyllic, and the distasteful were all part of the mix—not all that different from where I grew up or maybe from where you live. Food—a cultural, spiritual, and moral casserole. Welcome to the feast!

Forgetting Food, Forgetting God

We have cut ourselves off from the abundant life that God intends for all people. This is a most serious matter, for it goes to the nature and destiny of human life: to glorify God *and to enjoy* God forever![1] We have become disoriented and estranged from God, neighbor, and self. One glaring way we have forsaken abundant life is that we no longer fully appreciate or enjoy God's great gift of food. We have forgotten the purposes behind the blessing of food and have been satisfied with an impoverished appreciation of eating. Eating is a spiritual practice that reminds us of who we are in the global ecology. Forgetting what food is means we also forget who God is, who we are, and the nature of the world we inhabit.

There are two ways we suffer from failing to enjoy food and eating, and both are caused by disconnections. The first is that we Christians forget who is the giver of the gifts of food and eating. We forget the source of our food. To the extent that we are disconnected from enjoying food, we become disconnected from God. Food becomes mundane, a reality that slips beneath our notice. We may lose sight of the material reality of God's movement and care.

The second disconnection we experience in not enjoying food is that we lose a sense of relationship with other human beings and the earth. The majority of us who live in the United States and other affluent nations have become mindless to what all is involved in food—its production, preparation, enjoyment, and capacity to promote social bonding. Food is too routine, too easy, too cheap, too available for us to note what it represents and offers. We forget what it takes to grow and prepare food. We chase success in the midst of plenty. Satisfaction and enjoyment are readily available, but we race by our neighbors and by succulent meals too fast to see those possibilities. We have lost sight of God's greatest blessings—the earth and other humans, both of which nurture us.

A Worldview without Joy

Those of us in the affluent modern sector of the world have inherited a worldview that decreases the amount of enjoyment we experience—a view that sees life as a business to be managed and images ourselves as "skin-encapsulated egos."[2] The ego, of course, is that part of the self that manages the psyche and the self's activities. The phrase "skin-encapsulated egos" also notes the way we discount our bodies and fail to consider others, our bodies, or the earth as integral to who we are. To the extent that we incorporate this worldview, we understand ourselves primarily as individuals who, by managing the external affairs of the world and our relationships, can produce happiness. It is a worldview that touts the extent of human control and has much in common with an Enlightenment set of assumptions. It suggests that we can buy happiness and manage ourselves to generate a happy life.

Significant factors feed into the worldview that we can control our lives and ourselves. One does not have to look far to see how advertising employs base metaphors to encourage consumption, sending us the message that we can manage our lives and the environment. Advertising and marketing aim to make us feel dissatisfied with what we have—we can never have enough, and what we have can never be new enough. The sheer quantity of advertising that so many of us take in socializes us into this worldview.

The (over)work patterns of Americans are a second influential sector of our lives and also carry many of these same messages.[3] The long hours and increasing demands of work tend to foster in us an instrumental view of ourselves: oblivious to bodily stress and impervious to enjoyment. These work experiences remove us from the immediacy of bodily experience in the name of efficiency and performance.

The events of September 11, 2001, seem to have heightened our sense of the need to control our lives, even as they revealed our vulnerability. They have demonstrated just how much enjoyment depends on others and how hollow are the claims of what achievement and accomplishment can produce. Still, fear of what could happen and a distrust of others continues to affect our capacity to enjoy.

These examples bring into view yet another aspect of this worldview: the apprehension that scarcity lurks just beyond the present moment. Indeed, an economic downturn becomes a real cause for desperation. Yet, even when experiencing abundance, we feel we have to work hard to avoid calamity or other unhappiness.

In short, life is about business. At the root of this worldview is a mechanistic model of the self that divides life into separate components—work, family, religion, play, health, civic life, and friendship.

We have to be mindful of each area and make certain each is independently healthy and doing well; that is our understanding of well-being, of success.

This set of values and assumptions, so representative of a Protestant work ethic, proves counterproductive to enjoyment. Protestants feel vaguely guilty when they stop working a moment to relax and enjoy life. Such values emasculate our native abilities to feel, to sense, to encounter the world immediately. In times of economic prosperity the skin-encapsulated ego may be able to put off or manage his or her life "successfully," if without enjoyment. In times of crisis, however, this worldview creates feelings of powerlessness and despair. The promise of procuring happiness by following this path falls flat. We find ourselves enjoying our lives less than we thought we would.

An Alternative Worldview

An alternative view sees life basically as a matter of relationships. This relational model expresses the more abundant life that God intends for all God's creatures—a life in which meaning and happiness arise from relating to others, ourselves, and nature. Relationships, from this point of view, are intrinsically valuable rather than just instrumental. Such a model also connects our relationship with God with our potential for happiness.

Much of enjoyment is as mysterious as relationships. We cannot produce it; we simply have to appreciate it. There are many sources of enjoyment, however, and we can do much to experience those source. We can open ourselves to enjoy our lives and can encourage others to enjoy theirs as well. All of us are connected to each other and to natural life in such a way that our enjoyment reinforces and increases that of others, and others' enjoyment increases ours. Thus we all have a stake in others' and our own enjoyment.

The base metaphor for this worldview, then, is that we are holistic creatures who live in and through a communal web. We are bodily as well as spiritually and mentally alive. Unhappiness is the result of being relationally estranged, disconnected, and disoriented. Happiness and well-being consist of a harmonious connection with other beings, God, and the world. Others are intrinsically valuable, and our own happiness is a by-product of being rightly related to them and to ourselves. There is no scarcity of that which produces happiness and fulfillment, and this view does not foster a mechanistic, managerial approach to life. How radical is that?

To be sure, in discussing these two worldviews as "alternatives" to each other, I have overdrawn the contrast. There are areas of life where a managerial, controlled style is both necessary and desirable—for example, areas where law is appropriate and needed. There are regions of the world and even parts of affluent countries where there is material scarcity that detracts from life itself. Work is not always drudgery; for many, work is fulfilling and meaningful. However, this contrast calls attention to what receives first priority: Are our lives primarily oriented to management or to relationships? Are our relationships in the service of individual planning (the business model) or is our individual planning in the service of relationships?

Food experiences provide an excellent case study for these contrasting worldviews. Eating is something we do everyday: we can either approach it as a task, something to get done, or we can approach it as an occasion for appreciation and enjoyment, something to be experienced.

BEGINNING WITH EXPERIENCE

Why is an exploration of food and eating integral to our happiness? We must begin, as we already have, with experience. We do this because we believe that God is present in and through the experience of eating, and that our theology needs to reflect an awareness of that natural goodness. This is important for believers who may not expect to find God active in such everyday or routine acts as eating. One of my colleagues says that most people in biblical times spent 90 percent of their time producing or preparing food; another talks about Jesus eating his way through the Gospel of Luke!

Too often our theology seems to deal only with distant abstractions; things like food and eating seem too mundane for theological treatment. Many people have had difficulty believing me when I have told them I am writing a theology and ethics of eating. I inter-

pret their quizzical looks (if not outright laughter) as an indication
that they don't really believe there is anything theological about eating. (But then, ironically, they almost invariably tell me food stories!)
God's blessings and grace are all around us, and we miss these signs
of God's grace because they are too mundane, too everyday, too present. This must pain God. After all, how do you feel when your gifts
are set aside?

When we begin with experience, theology loses its aura of dealing
only with remote, profound, and infrequent events or doctrines.
Indeed, our own experience counts, and counts a great deal, in this
theology of eating. Our own sense of religious experience is on the
front burner of this book, so to speak. Our experience of eating
becomes part of the subject matter of theology. Food and eating can
reveal the presence of God; they can also express the deepest values
of our community. I invite you to consider how God is present in the
food that you and I eat and the full experience of it.

An increasing number of theologians today begin with experience—especially women theologians and those writing from their
own experiences in developing countries. By writing their experiences of God's activity in the world, they call us to recognize where
God is active rather than make us "think God into the world" or
"apply" their theology to the world. Most Christians believe that
God is already present in the world. Thus, theology is a way of thinking about our religious experience of God.

Let me illustrate briefly. We could take the doctrine of resurrection to indicate only a belief in Jesus' resurrection or the resurrection
of the body in an age to come. However, feminist theologians suggest
that resurrection indicates the possibility of a new life that God
enables every day. Feminist theology suggests a renewed valuing of
bodily life in all its forms and calls on the church to be the bearer of
resurrection—to be the witness to the new life that is already
effected by Jesus Christ.[4] Christians have traditionally focused so
much on the ways bodily resurrection is "not yet" that they miss the
ways that it is already present. The celebration of eating may be one
way to celebrate the "already" of the bodily resurrection.

IMAGINATIVE EATING

Living the resurrection is an experience with powerful implications for how we live, including how we eat. The experience of new life is what resurrection is about. Similarly I hope that we might discover the sense of resurrection and blessing that accompanies eating.

Hans Georg Gadamer, a German philosopher, conceived of the relationship between experience and thought as the difference between dancing and talking about dancing. Gadamer pointed out that the meaning of dancing is, in the first place, in the dancing itself. Analogously, for us the first meaning of food is in the eating of it, in the experience and sensations of eating. In the second place, the dance's meaning resides in our ability to enter through imaginative empathy into the experience of others' dancing. For food and eating, this second meaning resides in our ability to imagine others' eating (or not eating). Only in the third place, and this derives from the other two, does the meaning of the dance consist of words that are spoken or written about it.[5]

The meaning of food, then, is to be found at a primal level in the experience of eating. A second level is our empathetic imagination of the other's eating. The third level, then, consists of trying to convey or think about the experience. My fear is that the foundational meaning of eating and drinking may be lost, both the experience of eating and also what Christians understand about food when they say grace or celebrate the Eucharist. Often theology moves to abstractions and loses the foundational experience. This would be equivalent to trying to describe a dance without ever having danced or without ever having entered empathetically into another's dancing. That is why I suggest that we, today, recover the fullness of the experience of eating, of saying grace, and of Eucharist.[6]

SAYING GRACE HABITUALLY

I confess that our family's everyday table blessing frequently becomes routine. We simply go through the motions when we sing, "Oh, the Lord's been good to me, and so I thank the Lord. . . ." But we don't really thank the Lord. We are not conscious of God's graciousness to us and the way Jesus Christ became an eater like us. However, even then, I want to hold on to traditions, because sometimes we can breathe new life into them. Sometimes I can rest in them when I am completely out of breath. In the writing of this book, I have become newly appreciative of food—its ultimate source in God and also its penultimate sources: earth and laborers, the people I share food with, and the concerns we bring to the table. I recognize and respect the world of those plants and animals that have contributed to my nurture and pleasure. In this way I become sensitive to God's grace and newly aware of my dependence on God, other people, and other beings. I am more attuned to grace while I am "saying" it.

Still, "saying grace" becomes fairly mundane at times. Even then (perhaps especially then), my wife reminds me, the forms themselves can carry us; they may prevent us from falling farther away from God. At other times we are more aware of grace in our lives by praying over the food, giving thanks, and asking for God's continued blessing. One of the reasons why saying grace becomes mundane is because we are seldom really hungry. This also accounts for our lack of attention to food and eating as a religious activity.

A Range of Hungers

Most Christians in the affluent, industrialized "First World" are seldom if ever hungry. In fact, many of us do not think of hunger as a normal human experience. The sort of hunger we may only occasionally feel is a gentle hint on a scale of negativity, which middle-class North Americans avoid at all costs.[7] Fortunately, it is impossible to avoid a sensation that we might identify as pre-hunger. This can make us aware of just how biological we creatures still are, and it allows us to enter into the experience of eating or not eating. It allows us to imagine hunger, to remember that hunger is a primary human experience. We can also enter empathetically into other people's experience of not eating or, indeed, of overeating. We know what eating is, even if our own experience of hunger does not awaken the empathy for not eating that an intense experience of hunger might.

Our hunger is natural, and it points to a number of other hungers. Hunger of any kind—for food, for companionship, for cultural stimulation, and so on—drives the human animal to search for that which we need (or, in the case of misguided drives, at least for what we think we need). To be sure, there are distorted hungers and clear legitimate and illegitimate limits to the satisfaction of hunger. Even in the case of distortion, however, hunger is a clue to genuine desire and to God-given appetites.

Basic hunger is functional; it drives us toward satisfaction. It is a global human experience. There is no immunity from hunger; without eating, a human being can only live for two or three weeks. The limit on lack of water is much shorter, four or five days. Hunger makes us aware of the degree of our dependence on the world of nature for food, air, and water. Hunger is painful, a fact that is difficult for us who are the comfortable to remember. Hunger can make people aware of their interdependence with other human beings and the institutions we have created. When we are frustrated, hunger can be brutalizing. It can begin to take over the rest of our lives.[8]

Hunger for food also expresses other physical needs—needs for warmth, shelter, clothing, sleep, and touch. We hunger to meet other nonphysical needs: a life of companionship with other human beings, animals, and the world of nature. We hunger for freedom from fear, for human dignity, for some voice in our future, for sex, beauty, and security.[9]

Hunger and Desire

Often we fail to see desire or appetite as an asset. However, hunger reveals the centrality of desire for well-being. Never to be hungry mutes the place of appetite, and with it the positive way that appetite lifts into consciousness the role of that for which we hunger. Losing sensitivity to hunger for food may make it more difficult to recognize and deal with other kinds of hunger. It makes it difficult to understand oneself as a biological and emotional creature.

There has been a groundswell of Christian theological thought about the role of desire. Leon Kass, a philosopher and chair of the

President's Commission on Bioethics, suggests that appetite, desire, and longing are integral to human nature and, as he puts it, "Appetite or desire, not DNA, is the deepest principle of life."[10] Kass's account looks first not to eating *customs* as a clue to the perfecting of our nature but "to *nature*, to the meaning of what is naturally given to us as human beings, here and everywhere, now and always: our need for food. . . . [T]he testimony of our own lived experience can provide a royal road to appreciating what we are and discovering what we might become."[11] Kass finds appetite, longing, and desire to be "the spur to all aspiration, to action and awareness, to having a life at all. Bodies as incorruptible as diamonds, or bodies beyond themselves, would have no impulse or orientation to the world beyond their borders. . . . Here, in the germ of hunger, is the origin of all the appetites of the hungry soul"[12] Kass also identifies food as relational. His perspective is exciting because it arises from natural experience and reveals the "germ" of hunger that ranges from material need to the need for love in a way that elevates the material and concretizes the metaphysical. Kass's perspective implies at base a deeply religious, incarnational theology.[13]

The recent work of Michelle Lelwica, *Starving for Salvation: The Spiritual Dimensions of Eating Problems among American Girls and Women*, suggests that the pain and suffering that is associated with hunger can be a first step toward recognizing and beginning to counter those dynamics that lead to eating disorders.[14] To be sure, the intense hunger that precedes starvation is nothing to be celebrated. Nevertheless, the point here is that we should attend to our desires, our hungers, and our longings not only to fulfill or satiate them and certainly not to misidentify distorted appetites as "hungers." Instead, we need to attend to our hungers to examine our deepest needs and nature and be able to identify where appetite ends and greed begins. Otherwise, we will continue to live with unsatisfied appetites rather than being happy. We need to locate and prioritize our authentic hungers so that we might learn how to live together in a way that respects each other and the rest of the natural world. That sort of respect and appreciation can be thought of as an impulse toward worshiping God. The world of eating is one ground-level experience that can open onto these vistas.

OUR DEEPEST HUNGER

Our deepest hunger, our greatest need, is "to be called forth into the fullness of being," which Monika Hellwig, a Roman Catholic moral theologian, calls "creative love," and which can be thought of as wholeness or salvation. This need "often makes itself felt in a hunger to be worthwhile, to be valued or appreciated, to have a purpose or goal in life."[15] Hunger for a "creative love" is hunger for a force so grounded and grounding that the person can give as well as receive. Creative love supports accountability, weathers criticism, and directs one's life holistically. It calls for sharing and living in conscious dependence, for people to be fully alive and flourishing. It emerges in people who have such a sense of personal worth and meaning that they can share with others.

The Christian image of what it is to be fully human is found in the life, death, and resurrection of Jesus Christ. Especially in the image of Christ crucified for all created beings, voluntarily giving his life for all, Christians locate the redemption of all life. As Hellwig puts it, "this is why we are able to find there [in self-giving] the key to the redemption of the world from its self-maintaining cycle of hungers and oppressions."[16]

GOD'S GRACE AND OUR HUNGERS

Clearly, hunger is an important guide to our well-being and enjoyment. It directs us, through desire, to that authentic creative love that belongs, in the first place, only to God. God has communicated that love to us in the person of Jesus Christ. Celebrating the Lord's Supper is an invitation into Jesus' death and resurrection. It is no coincidence that this invitation comes at the table that meets our deepest hunger. This table also celebrates our ability to give—to live out to some extent the gracious giving-ness of God—and thus express hope for the whole world.

It is a great mystery to me that "only in hungering and thirsting after righteousness" shall I be filled (Matt. 5:6). Or that only by losing myself, by giving myself, that I will find myself. Indeed, God has arranged our hungers in such a way that in them we can see God's intention in both creation and also what has been revealed most fully in the life, death, and resurrection of Jesus Christ. The claim that sharing and self-giving is the way of redemption is a mystery. It is also quite countercultural, especially in light of the presiding mechanistic worldview in our society. If Jesus had advised hoarding food or eating only with one's friends, that our culture can understand! We can only glimpse the mystery of our great hungers for food and for creative love, which underwrite the world. We worship the Father, Son, and Spirit who designed and continue to design our world. Trying to pretend to unravel this mystery is perhaps as dangerous as ignoring it. This book will try to maintain that tension.

What we do know is that food and eating are important avenues toward understanding God's presence in the world. Food and eating can satisfy our hungers in such a way that they lead to that creative love that issues in deepest enjoyment and joyful sharing.

God's Intention
for Food

The lyric of abundance asserts that because the world is held in the hand of the generative, generous God, scarcity is not true. . . . The claim of creation faith is that there is more than enough to share, and where there is sharing there is generativity of more, because as the fruitful instruments of creation notice the *shalom* of God enacted as sharing, they do in fact produce more.

—Walter Brueggemann
The Covenanted Self

We might recall that Jesus was labeled by his detractors as a "glutton and a drunkard." And we may try to imagine the joyful occasions that called forth that charge. Indeed, Jesus had the temerity to suggest that the table-fellowship shared with disciples, tax-gatherers, and sinners constituted an anticipation of the Kingdom of God. He proclaimed the presence of the Kingdom in the eating and drinking and talking and laughing of those occasions.

—Bruce T. Marshall

IT WAS HIGH SUMMER in Eastern Iowa. Along the Mississippi River are bluffs on either side and, further in, valleys surrounded by ridges. In July the days seem endlessly beautiful and the legendary rich soil produces forests as green as the cornstalks. Some days seem almost archetypal; they are the way days were meant to be. This was one of those days.

My friends Lyle and Rachel live on Terrell Ridge, a place where you can fall in love with the local topography. Lyle is an old farm boy who knows plants. He moved from town to Terrell Ridge to have some acreage to farm. His intentions show in the size and lusciousness of his garden. Between the expected Silver Queen corn and cabbages and rhubarb and onions there are marigolds and zinnias and bok choy and plants I can't recognize.

Sometimes you do pick the right evening to eat outside. Other friends Marsha and Ann were joining us, and Rachel had been marinating the chicken for the barbecue since last night. The charcoal was all red. It was just too nice not to eat outside.

Our contribution was margaritas—made well, not hurried, with limes and tequila. Marsha brought a big salad and Ann a key lime pie. Nothing was terribly fancy but all of it had been made with care in anticipation of good friends eating together.

We ate next to the almost-farm-sized garden as the warm sun lingered as long as possible on top of the ridge. The beauty of the plants intensified the goodness of the food on our plates. I have forgotten what we talked about, but the conversation was lively. I do remember the sense of flow that pervaded the whole evening, which was just short of being too good—*perfecto,* as the Italians would say.

What Makes Eating Good?

You doubtless remember experiences of eating well, just like the one I have described. What made these experiences memorable for you? What is it that turns an ordinary meal into one that you recollect again and again? There are some features—such as eating with friends and great weather and a beautiful natural setting and delicious food—that combine to lift the experience out of the norm.

While these experiences of eating well relate to the Christian life, that does not yet establish them as specifically Christian. It is important to avoid simply identifying what feels good with being Christian. There are notorious incidents of people too easily equating their own preferences or commitments with God's. The Christian tradition is quite clear about people's disposition toward sin, toward presuming in favor of their own well-being and against their neighbors'. This makes all the more vital a willingness to "test the spirits" (1 John 4:1), to measure the apparent goodness of an experience by criteria other than whether it pleases our senses.

The experience of eating so pervades our lives that it practically demands reflection. What makes for healthy eating? This is a spiritual question: how can we eat to the glory of God? How do we know that God is present in our experience of eating? How can we know that our style of eating is pleasing to God? Few experiences go uninterpreted; our human capacities push us to reflect on our past experiences and project them into the future.[1] One habit or virtue that Christians develop is the ability to ask whether some experience is or is not in line with God's purposes. An example is the recent "WWJD" fad—wearing bracelets to remind ourselves to ask, "What Would Jesus Do?"This is a way some Christians make decisions and evaluate their experiences.

Scripture has long been seen as the primary authority and as a way to locate the presence and will of God.[2] Since Scripture is a faith-account of how God relates to humans and other creatures, men and women interpret events in juxtaposition to such transcendent criteria. They also intend to embody in their actions and style of acting those qualities that are in accord with God's will.

To be sure, Scripture is not a sufficient guide to the Spirit's inbreaking revelation; we expect revelation to be ongoing. But seldom is such revelation at odds with the primary thrusts of Scripture.[3] The interpretation of Scripture, in preaching or Bible study groups or private devotions, enables us to evaluate whether our experience is of God or not. We can say, on the basis of Scripture, that this or that activity is Christlike; it is responsive to God's activity and reflects qualities that are endorsed by Scripture. We can be wrong, we can change our minds, we can modify our manner of acting, we can learn and grow. But we cannot do without the witness of Scripture.

What follows is an interpretation, an effort on my part to locate in Scripture what God has to say about food and eating. Further, what does the experience of God's people, and especially the incarnation of Jesus Christ, have to say to us about eating?

The Old Testament

We begin with the Hebrew Scriptures, or Old Testament, which is replete with concrete, down-to-earth themes that relate to food and eating. These faith-accounts no doubt informed Jesus' understanding of food and eating practices. They also uncover for us aspects of God's relations to the Hebrew people that involve food.

One way to look at the Old Testament is to see the series of covenants that Yahweh made with humankind. A covenant exhibits Yahweh's way of relating to the people of Israel. The covenants range from an implicit covenant with humankind at creation to the covenant with Noah, with Abraham, the Deuteronomic covenant with Moses, the Judges, David, Solomon, and up to the new covenant incarnate in Jesus Christ. Through these covenants God promised to take the initiative in providing many benefits. In response, the people of Israel were to obey the *Torah* (or law) of Yahweh, for example, by "loving the LORD your God, walking in his ways, and observing his commandments . . ." (Deut. 30:16). *If* the people did obey Yahweh, they were promised long life, blessings, productive land, and good food.

For our purposes, we can think in terms of the two parties to these covenants. The witness of the Old Testament is that God acted in certain characteristic ways that carry an authority that human beings were to recognize. Miroslav Volf calls this the "as-so" structure or logic; *as* God acts and relates to human beings, *so* are human beings to relate to each other and the world.[4] Human beings, for their part, are to respond to God's action by acting in accord with God's law. We can therefore trace some of the central themes relating to food by dividing them in two ways: God's initiative and human response.

GOD'S INITIATIVE

Israel understood Yahweh to be the initiator of the covenantal relationship. Just in case anyone were to miss that affirmation, Hebrew Scripture begins with God's creation and our first covenantal theme: the earth, and especially food, are part of *created goodness*. In Genesis 1:29, human beings are given "every plant yielding seed" and "every tree with seed in its fruit; you shall have them for food"; in verse 30 the animals, birds, creeping things, and *every* breathing being are "given every green plant for food." "And God saw everything that he had made, and indeed, it was very good" (Gen. 1:31).[5]

It is quite clear that the Hebrew people believed that Yahweh had provided good food for humans and animals. The subject of food receives explicit treatment in the creation accounts. It is essential to notice that God creates in such a way that all beings are given food, a covenant that is expanded when God gives meat to Noah and his previously vegetarian descendants to eat (Gen. 9:3-4). Here we see the beginnings of Jewish dietary laws, which prohibited humans and animals from eating blood.

Food and all life, then, are created good, and the whole of creation works together to make for the good of each. The covenant promise reiterated throughout the Old Testament is that God the Divine Gardener will continue to nurture and supply our needs with loving care. Food, health, and our very lives are good gifts. Old Testament scholar Walter Brueggemann, in his commentary on Genesis, reminds us of the need to make visible linkages between the "overpowering miracle of creation" and the "daily reality of food." One way of doing this is by saying grace. In the table grace, Brueggemann says, we acknowledge that we "live by grace and know that we are strangely sustained, nurtured, and nourished."[6] We are mysteriously gifted by food from God; this brings into view the mystery of our complex selves and our need to live by grace rather than by grasp.

A second strong initiative by God is the *blessing* that God bestows on men and women. This is a central tradition in the Old Testament that points to the routine ways—such as the blessing of food—by which God has graced our lives.[7] Not as dramatic or as conspicuous as other biblical traditions that focus on the historical acts of God, the blessing tradition is one that celebrates the cycles of nature, the role of family, and all that sustains and regularly enriches our everyday enjoyment. These blessings are not measured out by scarcity but by abundance.[8] They are represented as overflowing:

Surely goodness and mercy shall follow me
    all the days of my life,

and I shall dwell in the house of the LORD
  my whole life long. (Ps. 23:6)

All meals were understood as blessings.

The abundance of this blessing and the frequency with which food is celebrated in connection with it reveal the Israelite understanding that food is sacramental, a sign of God's blessing. "In the Old Testament," writes Sara Juengst, "the sacred character of food is both explicit (as when it is used for sacrifices) and implicit (as in the Leviticus laws governing eating). Its sacredness is evident in its being a part of the covenant promise: '[the Lord] provides food for those who fear him;/ he is ever mindful of his covenant'" (Ps.111:5; see also Lev. 26:3-5).[9]

HUMAN RESPONSE

The covenant requires human response to God's initiatives of created goodness and blessing. Understanding food as created good, a blessing, and a gift from God leads to a central aspect of human response: appreciation. In response to Yahweh's gift, the creatures are to enjoy that gift; they are to celebrate, feast, and party. The delight that humankind and others take in God's goodness breaks out in playfulness (Psalm 104, Eccles. 9:7), in trees clapping their hands (Isa. 55:12), and in worship (Ps. 144:9-15).

A cycle of feasts in the Israelite religious year celebrated food and other blessings in this way. Perhaps most remarkable is the tone of exuberance that pervades the response to Yahweh. The joy, the delight that is expressed in appreciation is the primary, foundational level of response. Our overflowing appreciation of this gift increases its enjoyment and our desire to ensure the continuation of healthy food and a healthy earth for the future. We are stewards of self as well as of others—to God's glory.[10]

Another dimension of appreciation, as we all know, is sharing food with others. This is the sort of commensality or mutuality that my wife and I shared with Lyle, Rachel, Marsha, and Ann on that idyllic summer evening described earlier. We came together to eat. Eating seals the bonds of friendship as it expresses and generates

intimacy with others. It is difficult to imagine any genuine community whose members never eat together. Part of appreciation, then,
is sharing with friends, all the while forging and deepening the
bonds of friendship.

While we speak of hospitality in conjunction with social occasions,
the Old Testament injunction of *hospitality* to strangers was part of
the Yahwist religion. Whether or not it was because hospitality was
vital to life among nomadic peoples, as Old Testament scholar Philip
King suggests, there are nevertheless clear illustrations of and injunctions to hospitality in the Hebrew Scripture.[11] The two obligations of
hospitality are to feed and to protect the stranger or guest. The practice of hospitality is a sacred duty emanating from the awareness that
God is the generous host of us all. We are the slave people whom Yahweh delivered from Egypt and thus "you shall not oppress the alien";
rather, "you shall love the alien as yourself; for you were aliens in the
land of Egypt: I am the LORD your God" (Lev. 19:33-34).

Hospitality became an expression of the covenant relationship
with God and with human beings.[12] Through our hospitality, we imi-
tate the love and generosity of God. We respond to God's hospitality
by exhibiting *compassion and justice* to all. We are especially to
insure that the hungry are fed, that unjust distributions of wealth are
adjusted, that the land is protected, that justice is done, and that the
outcast is welcomed at table. Though there is a place for fasting, Isaiah speaks for Amos, Jeremiah, and Hosea when he prophecies:

> Is not this the fast that I choose: to loose the bonds of
> injustice, to undo the thongs of the yoke, to let the
> oppressed go free, and to break every yoke?Is it not to share
> your bread with the hungry, and bring the homeless poor
> into your house; when you see the naked, to cover them,
> and not to hide yourself from your own kin? (Isa. 58:6-7;
> see also Jer. 7:4-5; Hos. 6:6; Amos 5:21,14)

Part of the sin of gluttony is that it is a form of greed, an obsession
with self, and an ignoring of the plight of others. Gluttony has no part
in the compassion for others that motivates justice. (Nor is gluttony
ultimately even self-satisfying.)

Before we turn to the New Testament, one last Old Testament body of material deserves attention—the dietary laws of the Torah. Philosopher Leon Kass turns to these laws to explore how they "[stand] between humankind and the divine" and how relationship gets incorporated into food customs and practices.[13] He contends that the dietary laws aim not only to ennoble but also to *sanctify* eating. These laws are memorials to creation. They remind human eaters of their dependence upon nature while also reminding them of the problematic character of eating—the way that eating can be a threat to life. The concern of the Jewish dietary laws is holiness, the maintenance of right relations. We are to be holy, to become sanctified by obeying these laws in recognition of the mysterious source of our lives, and by imitating God's wisdom in making distinctions, for example, between that which is clean and that which is unclean. What Kass is saying here is that eating involves holiness; we can eat in a sanctified or holy manner—or not. By recovering the deeper meaning of eating, he says, "we can relearn the true relations to the formed world that the hungering soul makes possible."[14]

The New Testament

As we turn to the new covenant actualized in Jesus of Nazareth, the Son of God, the very first thing to say is that the themes we have identified thus far are the same that informed Jesus' understanding of eating. Jesus grew up among the themes of Hebrew Scripture and the dietary laws. Early in his ministry, according to the Gospel of Matthew, Jesus said, "Do not think that I have come to abolish the law or the prophets; I have come not to abolish but to fulfill" (Matt. 5:17).There is, of course, a different understanding of God's covenant in Jesus Christ that bears upon the manner in which dietary laws are viewed.But still, Jesus' teachings reinforce rather than eviscerate the understandings we have developed here.

Take the theme of appreciation, a significant and even foundational theme. Within the context of the old covenants, the theme of appreciation underlies the Torah regarding dietary, tithing, and justice practices. Nevertheless, to some extent the motive of gratitude behind these practices can be lost, and the practices can evolve into mere obligations or laws, disconnected from the framework of covenant. Within the frame of the new covenant established in Jesus Christ, however, this is not the case. Because God's love is expressed in a covenant not dependent upon human response, we can resist allowing our response to degenerate into reluctant obligation. The exuberance of God's covenant and God's overflowing love revealed in creation is preeminently manifest in the life, death, and resurrection of Jesus the Christ.

In fact, the motive for responding appreciatively to all that God has provided intensifies with the new covenant. However, there are additional important themes relating to eating and drinking that Jesus' life and teachings bring to light. The two themes are sufficiently distinct that I count them as additions: Eucharist (or the Lord's Supper), and mission. The other three and their Old Testament correlates (in parentheses) are: trust in God's providence (created goodness and blessing); feasting (appreciation and stewardship); and table fellowship (hospitality, compassion, and justice). We begin with themes that express God's initiative.

GOD'S INITIATIVE

The Old Testament themes of the created goodness of food and the blessings God bestows with food and drink prefigure Jesus' trust in God's providence. God has provided all that we need; thus Jesus enjoins his disciples to trust God's goodness. Indeed, Jesus almost rebukes the disciples: "Therefore do not worry, saying, 'What will we eat?' or 'What will we drink?' or 'What will we wear?' For it is the Gentiles who strive for all these things; and indeed your heavenly Father knows that you need all these things. But strive first for the kingdom of God and his righteousness, and all these things will be given to you as well"(Matt. 6:31-33).Clearly God has provided in the past and can be trusted into the future.[15]

Another Old Testament echo of God's providence is the way God supplied manna to the people of Israel in the wilderness, but only on a daily basis. This connects with the petition in the Lord's Prayer, immediately following the request that the kingdom come on earth as in heaven, that the Lord "give us this day our daily bread" (Matt. 6:11, Luke 11:2).Jesus taught the disciples to trust God for daily provision. Luther commented that this petition means we should trust and praise God for daily provision and not attempt to lay up treasures on earth.

In the New Testament feeding and healing stories, especially the feeding of the 5,000, we find proof of God's empathic providence. What more could one expect? Indeed, how could one even imagine such abundant providence? The exclamation drawn from the healing stories might be "Only by faith!" There is also an element of promise in these stories because Jesus seems to be demonstrating that God can be trusted to provide. The element of promise comes again to the fore in the parables of the messianic banquet.

The second theme of God's initiative—*Eucharist*—illustrates the nourishing character of food. The Eucharist or Lord's Supper captures so many of the themes that have to do with eating and drinking that it threatens to overwhelm all the rest. To avoid that, we focus here only on the essentials of the ritual as found in the New Testament, leaving more explicit theological treatment to the next chapter.

Jesus celebrated the Passover meal with his disciples shortly before his crucifixion. At that meal he expanded the understanding of the traditional feast of Exodus deliverance to include participation in the new covenant in his blood. The early church celebrated this ritual communally, both as a remembrance and as a covenant renewal.[16] Though the church has interwoven the ritual with many layers of meaning, we can nevertheless point with confidence to several specific themes.

The meal was understood as *eucharista*, as thanksgiving for the bounty that God had lavishly provided. Tied into daily food and drink was feasting with Jesus. There was a doxological or glorifying character to the meal, which was to pervade the life of the believer. Eucharist was an eating and drinking with Jesus who was providence *par excellence*. Yet, the significance of the act of eating and drinking should not be dismissed as merely the occasion for God's providence, not just the vehicle for the ritual. The celebration at the table marks, at the least, a deepening of the meaning of the everyday grace of God. Could it be that all eating is sacramental?

We find references throughout the Synoptic Gospels and indeed throughout the New Testament to this last meal. Luke in particular links eating and drinking with the proclamation of the kingdom, Jesus' central message. For example, Jesus calls the Pharisees to repentance at the banquet Levi the tax collector throws for Jesus (Luke 5:27-32). Some have even argued that it was Jesus' manner of eating that got him killed; Jesus defied sabbath laws and authorities by eating with people who were considered disreputable. To the extent that the Last Supper was the apex of eating and drinking, we can see in it the exemplification of what our material life was and is meant to include, that is, redemption. Eating with Jesus is the epitome of all that is present, symbolically and literally, in food and eating.

Especially in the apostle Paul's correspondence, we find an eschatological element in the Eucharist. According to New Testament scholar John Koenig, "Paul's view of the Lord's Supper as an eschatological feast, anticipating the kingdom, almost certainly coincided with what the earliest believers in Jerusalem thought about their ritual meal."[17] Into the Lord's Supper, then, there enters a visionary element focused toward the future. Participants express both a belief linking them to God's future and a commitment to acts of God's redemption. The World Council of Churches' document "Baptism, Eucharist, and Ministry" states: "As participants in the eucharist, then, we prove inconsistent if we are not actively participating in this ongoing restoration of the world's situation and the human condition. . . . The eucharist opens up the vision of the divine rule which has been promised as the final renewal of creation, and is a foretaste of it. . . ."[18]

HUMAN RESPONSE

The Eucharist is a God-initiated feast to which we respond. The feast that God has set before us invites us to *feast in appreciation*. Communion was instituted, many authorities think, at the Passover feast Jesus celebrated with his disciples. Clearly the early believers continued the tradition of feasting that weaves through the history of Israel as recorded in the Hebrew Scriptures.

The religious nature of many feast days—Christmas, Easter, Mardi Gras—has become diluted in the contemporary Christian church. For some reason, Thanksgiving comes closest to engendering a real sense of feasting as a religious activity. What is threatened by the loss of real feasting and its separation from religious origins is a sense of exuberant enjoyment that expresses appreciation and engenders stewardship. If the language of feasting is used of Eucharist and the only edible evidence of that is a bit of bread and a sip of wine, then the "feasting" and an accompanying sense of deep appreciation are short-circuited indeed.[19]

In the Old Testament, religious feasts were occasions of corporate covenant renewal. Feasts were occasions for people to remember Yahweh's gracious acts on their behalf and to recommit themselves to the bonds of worship and kinship. These occasions included processions, music, dancing, eating meat (a rare occurrence), and drinking. Observance of the pilgrimage festivals—Passover, Unleavened Bread, the feasts of Weeks, the feast of Booths—continued into New Testament times.[20]

The feasts of Unleavened Bread, Weeks, and Booths all had to do with food—celebrating the firstfruits of grain and also the harvest. Perhaps in an agricultural society this was not surprising. What was emphasized, however, was God's participation in the growing process and, indeed, in the everyday life of material provision. Furthermore, the feasts themselves, besides *expressing* appreciation, *engendered* an appreciation that strengthened stewardship practices.

Further, the corporate nature of these feasts must have included most of the people in particular communities in Israel and the early church. That corporate sense of communal feasting is significant in a culture like our own where feasts tend to be more and more privately observed. Also, feasts that go corporately underappreciated, as in fact they are in our contemporary situation, can jeopardize the corporate sense of stewardship. The reversal of these trends—in the church especially—would be healthy.

Several passages that have to do with feasting point to the ultimate eschatological banquet—the last feast. Isaiah 25:6-9 pictures all peoples coming together to feast and to celebrate God's rule throughout the whole world. All are brought together to recognize God as king and each other as kin. God will bring all people deliverance and restoration as they feast together. New Testament visions have striking similarities. The Great Banquet parables of Matthew 22:1-10 and

Luke 14:15-20 have the host inviting all sorts of people to come to the feast. Those who come are the despised, the little people, and the underdogs. There are some surprises about whom God will invite, who will accept, and who will be excluded. Those who are usually not included—the marginalized and the dispossessed—seem to have an inside track at this feast.

Jesus' everyday practices reflected the nature of the messianic banquet that Matthew and Luke describe. One could never be certain just who one might find at table fellowship with Jesus. Jesus ate with everybody. That may be the most important feature of his eating practices—and one that caused him a lot of trouble. So when Jesus calls Levi, a tax collector, to follow him, Levi makes a great feast and invites many other socially despised tax collectors to the table (Luke 5:27-29; see also Matt. 9:9-13; Mark 2:13-17). The Pharisees are not pleased. They ask Jesus' disciples, "Why do you eat and drink with tax collectors and sinners?" (Luke 5:30). Prostitutes, Samaritans, lepers, the handicapped, the poor, the hungry, and others get included in that designation as "sinners" or outcasts. The upper classes and respectable people ate only with those of like status. For a religious leader like Jesus to associate with social dregs, even to the extent of social bonding at table, was offensive and unthinkable.

The radical inclusiveness of Jesus—the way Jesus even sought out those who were outcasts, misfits, and on the edge—cannot be missed. Theologian Sallie McFague makes a great deal of Jesus' practice of table fellowship in her designation of God as "friend."[21] Jesus was the friend of all. This same sort of inclusiveness carries the day when the Jerusalem church engaged in a conflict over who could be admitted to fellowship (see Acts 10 and 11). It is this basic equality of all believers that Paul says ought to characterize the Corinthians' agape feast (1 Corinthians 11–13), and which, in many other passages, Paul encourages the churches to develop.

In short, the concern for compassion and justice overwhelms the concern for respectability. Hospitality to the stranger and especially to the poor and needy are hallmarks of both the Old and New Testaments. The hospitality of table fellowship is the behavioral correlate of Jesus' compassion, his *splanchnizesthai* [Greek for "having a churning of the insides"]. This is the word that is used of Jesus' reaction to the destitute, the sick, and the hungry when they approach him. It leads to a concern to see that justice is done.

Theologian Marianne Sawicki goes even further. She asks how we can recognize the risen Lord and analyzes the Gospels of Matthew and Luke to this effect: "Talk about resurrection is literally meaningless in the absence of [action on behalf of the needy]. This raises the serious question of what it takes to speak correctly about resurrection. . . . Actions of justice not only transform human need into well-being; they also transform words about resurrection into understanding of the identity of Jesus."[22] We are called to share because that is what Jesus did (Matthew 25; James 5).

The eating and drinking practices of Jesus, his disciples, and early Christian communities were *mission* practices. They were integrally tied into the outreach, by proclamation and action, of Jesus and the early church. This is one of the conclusions to which we are led by our consideration of table fellowship and the banquets for the unwashed in Matthew 22 and Luke 14. The early Christians seem to have celebrated the feast of *eucharista* often, perhaps weekly. These were not occasions for narrow remembrance in private, but sometimes they were held for the sake of introducing others into the fellowship. Sometimes they were designed to promote believers' offering themselves into new ministries of witness and outreach. They were table rituals that defined the mission of the disciples, witnessing to God's redemption of the whole created order. They carried the gospel out into the world in a special way by generating and fueling outreach ministries.

According to John Koenig, participants understood these table rituals as "contributing to God's restoration of the whole created order, with their own praise and thanks playing a vital role."[23] These occasions of feasting served the earliest believers in their missionary activity in three ways: (1) they were foundational for shaping, renewing, and expressing the community's identity; (2) such feasting occasions were probably the settings for baptism and confirming new members into missional identity; and (3) they were ways to channel the believers' communion with God into daily life.[24] The liturgies of messianic feasting were ways of reaching out to witness to what God has done and was still doing. They were occasions to invite others to join the feast. And they were fun.

LOOKING OVER all these biblical themes, we discover that they tend to coalesce around two poles. One is the pole of enjoyment, providence, goodness, delighting.

The other is the pole of hospitality, justice, mission, sharing. Therefore, I believe these are the two purposes that God had in mind in creating food for eating, food for life.

Food and the Christian Experience

Chef Primo [Tony Shalhoub]: Here, taste, taste this.
Ann [Allison Janney]: (takes a spoonful) Oh, my God . . .
(breathily) . . . oh God . . .
Primo: It's good, huh?
Ann: O my God . . .
Primo: O my God is right. Now you know. To eat good food is to be close to God.

—From the film *Big Night*

God comes to feed us, to fill us, to love us. "God pervades the world in the same way as honey in the comb," says Tertullian. Abundant beyond our wildest hopes, this bread is everywhere before us, sweet, like honey in our mouths, given to sustain us.

—Douglas Burton-Christie

EACH OF US began with desire.

Hunger for food is one form of the experience of desire. It is a drive, and if it is fierce enough, it can saturate our thinking and indeed our whole being. The hunger for food and drink expands to include other hungers, which usually incorporate food as well. It may be that the sense of appetite is learned from our first experiences of hunger, and that desire itself includes a visceral and appetitive edge, no matter how sublimated or spiritualized it may seem. St. Augustine would have understood that.

The questions we bring to the experience of desire and of hunger are "Where is God in our eating, and how does one experience God in food?" It is interesting that the absence of food can reveal hunger's meaning as well or better than its abundance. We will explore this in a later chapter.

Here, however, we turn to an exploration of our experience. You remember that in chapter 1 we argued that experience has to be tested to determine if it is inspired by the Spirit. How is God present in several of our experiences—in this case, hunger and eating? Just because an experience pleases us or feels good or satisfies our sense of beauty or morality is not sufficient to determine whether it is of Christ—Christian. Sometimes the ugly or sinful or disruptive or repulsive is a clue to how we should act. Our duty is not always pleasant.

For example, when our family was in Washington, D.C. (it could have been any large city), we passed a bundle of rags that used to be blankets lying on a grate every morning and every night. Our twelve-year-old was aghast to discover that this bundle was a person sleeping. This was not a pleasant, beautiful, satisfying experience for him or us; and it is possible, one could say, that we should therefore ignore our experience or just not attend to the person. Such neglect and lack of compassion would, of course, be a less than Christian response. Noticing, taking care, feeling compassion, addressing this man and others in similar situations of destitution seems far more in keeping with Christ's teachings. Our experience of good feelings or satisfaction or being pleased is not a very good guide to how we should respond as Christians. Of course the strength of our feeling is itself something of a clue to the meaningfulness of the experience.[1]

Experience is not self-interpreting or transparent. Experience is not yet theology; we have to test our experience and discover its content. In asking whether an experience is of Christ, whether God is present there, or whether what we feel is the Spirit, we are acknowledging that there is something more that makes the experience normative. There is a quality, an insight, a truth even, in some experiences that makes them worth accentuating and remembering and, indeed, worth trying to reproduce in our other activities and experiences. How can we know that the quality that characterizes certain experiences is worthy of being emulated? And so we return to the question: How do we know that God is present in our experience of eating?

Why Consider Experience?

In chapter 2 we located several biblical themes that relate to food and eating. They will serve us well as we proceed because they are qualities and experiences of eating that other people have accentuated and identified as normative. They have identified them as ones in which God is present. Our Christian theological tradition helps us answer the question regarding whether a particular experience is a channel of God and of Christian revelation. We might even ask the question as to whether they are God-bearing.

However, though they have a primacy, biblical themes are not sufficient. In part, this is because every description of a biblical theme is in fact an interpretation. The very themes I lift up are selected out of my own sense of priorities. They are not neutrally selected nor can they claim total objectivity—whatever that may be—so there is already an implicit theology at work here. On the other hand, neither of these themes is just my interpretation, as though it were totally subjective. The themes selected in chapter 2 represent a specific socialization; they are themes whose history stretches back to ancient Israel. These themes have been continually tested since that time and can be confidently presented as relevant in the present and into the future. However, the question remains if I have interpreted them in the most appropriate way. What makes the study of theology so interesting—such as answering our question of where God is in the midst of the experience of eating—is that there is not a final answer. Interpretations can be more or less persuasive; the Bible is not completely self-interpreting.

In short, we have to interpret Scripture and experience together. For example, while writing chapter 2 and describing Old Testament themes that relate to eating, I noticed myself slipping into the editorial "we" and treating those themes as though they were applicable in the present without modification. They may well be applicable; certainly they deserve to be incorporated into our account. But they are also historical themes that have been abstracted or lifted out of one historical period and cannot, without examination, be integrated into another period. In the change from a largely nomadic Israelite society of centuries before Christ to an urban, postmodern society, themes change their meaning. Take the theme of hospitality, for example. At some points in the history of Israelite society it was literally a matter of life and death for a host to offer hospitality to a traveler who was without food or water. Clearly the meaning of this theme changes in a society where the need for hospitality does not seem as urgent and where there is an effort to hide poverty and need. The meaning of the theme also changes when the consequences of starvation or thirst are diffused throughout the society, and the public has come to see the government as the caretaker of last resort— and only the very last resort. These forces have taken operational but not moral responsibility out of the hands of individuals or faith groups. Hospitality may still be a matter of life or death.

Developing a "Working Theology"

The task of working out or articulating the meaning of the Bible and tradition in conversation with our experience and present understandings is the task of theology. An interesting turn that theology has taken in response to postmodernity is that theology itself is often seen as more flexible and less dogmatic. Indeed, in mainstream theology, the logical status of dogmatism, if not dogmatism itself, has been dissolved as an intellectual possibility. Most theology now holds that tradition and Scripture become means of helping us think about our lives; they can still be the source of revelation, but they are not merely a set of propositions that we believe by sheer force of will. But this does not render tradition and Scripture irrelevant. In a way, tradition and Scripture have become more significant because they are understood in a more practical way. They are valuable in helping us deal with the perennial and emerging questions of meaning and decision-making that lie close to the core of being human—questions of worship and of living morally.

This understanding of theology overlaps with what Sallie McFague calls a "working theology."[2] At first glance that phrase seems to indicate a form of doing theology that is more accountable to context and humbler about our human capacity for certainty in matters of faith. It indicates that our theology is in process, that is, it continues to "work" within the parameters of our human finitude. Thus, it is relative and limited. It works with "relative absolutes." But I see even more in that phrase now. I see that a "working theology" is also one that is performative; that is, it relates to the world and to me. It works because it makes sense of experience. It is continually developing—not, to be sure, in a way that is totally innovating at every moment or one that is unmindful of tradition and Scripture, but clearly one that is open to ongoing revelation. McFague writes: "Revelation is an insight about God and the world that changes your life."[3] We do not just assent to revelation; revelation changes who we are. It changes ordinary experience—the experiences of eating and drinking, of sexuality and exclusion, of seeing people sleeping on grates, and of feeling a bit of the starvation of others.

Revelation has the quality of being transformative and also expansive. "It appears to be the case," writes McFague, "that the strength of the illumination and encounter of revelation—its impact on one's personal life—become the basis for expanding it to be revelation for all."[4] Thus, by its nature insistent on change, revelation pushes toward action and enables us to see and feel the connections between all things. It also claims to be true and capable of being experienced as normative in general. A working theology, therefore, is continually in process, but it also presses its own viewpoint on the basis that this insight has power.

Getting Food on the Theological Table

Despite the experiential emphasis of this understanding of "working theology," many people will find it strange to talk about food and eating as matters of faith and theology. Food doesn't seem to be on the table for theological discussion.[5] If there is an upside to the current epidemic of fears about food safety (for example, bioterrorism, mad cow, listeria, botulism, E. coli contamination), it is that the quality of our food supply and the well-being of animals and plants have once again become conspicuous.[6] Food has become a very hot topic today—witness the movies, TV shows, books, and articles that center on food. From "The Iron Chef" to *Chocolat* to newspaper debates on obesity, food is everywhere.

If that conspicuousness is seen as only a secular agenda, however, we will have lost a significant opportunity. The present offers a moment when Christians and others might be open to the religious significance of food and eating.

Conversely, it will be important for us to understand why food has seldom been seen as a theological matter. In this section my interest is in locating those areas of underbrush that have to be cleared before the constructive work of naming how God is involved in food and eating. This prior job is vital to that. The question is how God got dissociated from food in the first place.

No less an authority than Harvard theologican Gordon Kaufman uncovers a primary reason for this.[7] Kaufman points out that the Christian theology of the past two or three centuries has focused on *human* subjectivity, especially the subjectivity of death, pain, and suffering, and on how God addresses the existential or personal questions that face humankind. It paid little attention to the physical and natural world, whether nonhuman or human. Thus, it has come to pass that theology has been less capable of addressing the objective question of what we were doing to our biosphere. That simply hadn't been within the scope of our focus until the last thirty years or so. Kaufman writes: "So it is not really evident that God (as Christians have traditionally understood God) provides a solution to what is a major problem for men and women today: the ecological crisis."[8] His fundamental insight—that theology has underemphasized the involvement of God in the nonhuman world—is right on target. He suggests that we reconsider human beings as essentially *biohistorical*.[9] While this is a remedial direction, I believe it is only a half step when a whole step is needed. His definition still conceives of the physical and material world, which is part of what human body-selves are, as more or less self-contained and separate. In short, the physical (the bio-logical) is not the source of delight or a means of revelation and grace but only fodder for human management and control. I fear this way leads to destruction. It valorizes control too much when what is primordially needed is a foundation pointing toward the mutual connection of humankind and other life forms, and a description of the physical as interpenetrating all human mental and spiritual as well as physical processes. The physical and material should be seen as entering integrally into the historical and cultural (though quite limited) transcendence of humankind.

For example, why has theology seldom if ever considered the meaning of the fact that men and women defecate and urinate? I know, leave that alone, you say. Exactly. And that is what we have done to sexuality and also to economics and other topics, until recently. They are linked, to varying degrees, with the physical and material world. The fact that we are uncomfortable with God's involvement in these more objective worlds reinforces Kaufman's basic point.

Food and eating are, of course, intimately bound up with bodily processes. They reveal that we are in fact finite and mortal and limited. There is an unconscious circumvention around them.[10] One way to circumvent dealing with food and eating—and all that they imply about our connection to animal life and the limits on our technological control—is to dismiss the matters of food and eating as below the threshold of theological visibility. Of course to do that squelches a nemesis that reemerges to distort and truncate one's theology. This nemesis subverts arguments about sexuality, the power of economics in the church, and our quite-physical ecological niche, as though they did not enter theological debate. The anguish and gnashing of teeth this has produced in the debate by Christian churches about homosexuality in the past two decades is exhibit number one!

Our neglect of the implications of material life has been swept under the rug by discounting material life itself. There are deep roots to this neglect, but generally they are associated with a disconnection between the physical and the spiritual, where the spiritual is seen as superior to the physical.[11] The physical or material constitution of humankind—our very bodies—are seen as lacking spiritual meaning. This almost denies the importance of our incarnate, God-created material selves. It also denies the value of nature and of such central aspects of material life as sexuality and economics. So, for example, eco-theology is a product only of the last thirty years.

The costs of this neglect are brought home when we consider the impression that is left by our manner of "celebrating" Eucharist. The Lord's Supper is, at base, quite material about eating and drinking, which of course had its origin in a supper hosted by Jesus. However, when food and eating are discounted, the meal becomes a matter, according to biblical scholar Marcus Barth, where it is "only individual salvation and personal satisfaction that is sought, communicated, and actually experienced . . . so much restricted to the soul or to a life after death that little or no attention is paid to the body, to the present plight and needs of human society."[12]

What is in constant danger of being lost is precisely what men and women are closest to and can most readily understand: their own bodies and the simple experiences of eating and drinking together. Unfortunately, rather than being a means of grace, human bodies and their capacity for enjoyment are often left behind. Furthermore, the joy of eating and drinking together with others, which begs to be extended to all persons, is limited to individual satisfactions. By being divorced from the Eucharist's implications for our corporate life, the way we celebrate it enables us to blind ourselves to our ecological and material constitution. The fullness of the Lord's revelation is thereby blocked or missed.

Theological Models

In what ways and with what language can we talk about how God is in fact involved in the material world—especially the world of food and eating? Christians claim that God is actively involved in the world. There are two models for talking about God's activity that frame the options: *theist* and *determinist*. Neither model is adequate, but they frame the playing field and therefore are useful.

Theism and Determinism

The theist model images God's relation to the world as an absentee landlord who has merely left an agenda for men and women to follow. This theist (or *deist*) position represents one end of the pole as God may be seen as only occasionally involved—for example, at creation or the incarnation. So the theist might maintain that God set up the conditions for growing food (creation), and it is now up to humanity to manage the global food system and the environment. The determinist model sees God as being so active in the world that human beings are deluded when they claim that their actions are free in any sense whatsoever; therefore our lives lack any seriousness. This polar-opposite model would see God as growing and managing the contemporary global food system himself. Obviously these models go beyond simply talking about God's activity; they contain an image of human and ecological activity as well.

Recall my earlier claim that food tends to be seen in merely descriptive and functional terms in the contemporary world. Our intellectual history largely supports this understanding, which is tied to the theist model. The associated anthropology and worldview see humankind as transcending its environment, rather than being a part of its environment. The model that supports the view of food-as-fuel is mechanistic and scientific; it understands men and women as managers or controllers of the world and is linked to a technological rationality that manages the natural world for the benefit of humankind. Acting in continuity with this model will assuredly be destructive for future generations of all species.

With reference to food, this theistic-scientific model emphasizes the importance of managing one's diet, balancing nutrients, controlling one's intake, and making food affordable and safe. On a global scale, it attempts to do the same, only bigger and broader. It appears to be Christian, but the God it models is mostly an empty concept. This is an ahistorical notion of God rather than the personal God of Scripture who acts in quite specific ways and demonstrates particular values. This is the theist God of civil religion, which can be used ideologically to support any sort of political, economic, or scientific goal that we fix upon.

This model leaves humankind in the driver's seat. But, as history has shown us, our driving is erratic and collision-prone.

INCARNATIONAL MODELS: ALEXANDRINE AND ANTIOCHENE

If we reject the theist option and regard the determinist model as not deserving serious consideration, then what other ways can we image the activity of God in regard to food and eating? Fortunately we have clear alternatives that derive from the incarnation. Christians claim that God became flesh and was actively present in the person of Jesus Christ. Therefore, if we are concerned to say how *God* is present in the world, we could look to models of how *Christ* was present to give us some guidance.

There are two options here: the Alexandrine and the Antiochene models. These options date back to the patristic era in church history and represent two schools of thought, each of which has generated different ways of conceiving the activity of God in the world. They will both be useful to us.

The Alexandrine Model

The distinction between the two models hinges on the question of how the divine and the human are related. The Alexandrine model of Christology maintained that the two natures of Christ—the divine and the human—should be carefully kept discreet. This model is concerned that the blurring of the human and the divine be seen as a denigration of the supreme majesty of God. Both Clement of Alexandria and, later, Origen maintained a transcendent image of God as immutable and ineffable, underscoring the distance between the Godhead and the material world. Thus, when explaining how humankind is created in the image of God, Origen insisted that this does not in any way refer to the body, but to the intellectual and spiritual nature of the human being, which is "incorporeal, invisible, incorruptible, and immortal." Furthermore, Origen identified the "vanity" to which the world is subject as "nothing else than the body."[13]

Jesus Christ thus becomes the divine intermediary between God and man, the immutable and the mutable, and is God-man as the revelation of God. The sacraments, then, tend to become illustrative of spiritual realities. According to this view, the finite is not capable of the infinite, and thus in the Lord's Supper the bread and wine do not in any manner become the body and blood of Christ.

A legitimate fear behind the development of Alexandrine ways of thinking was that the human would get confused with the divine and lead to a worship of false gods. There is a great deal of reliance upon human reason and external revelation in this model of Christology. When it comes to ethics, questions that emerge from this model attempt to locate the purpose and will of the transcendent God, manifesting a tendency to trust one's head more than one's heart.[14]

Regarding an ethics of eating, the question we would ask of this theology is: "What are the purposes of God for food and eating?"

The Antiochene Model

The second model, the Antiochene, is less concerned about keeping the two natures of Christ separate and more concerned about making sure that the two are seen as conjoined: Jesus was both divine and human at the same time. For Irenaeus, who can be identified as the progenitor of this model, the issue is not separation, but union. He speaks of a God "whose very hands enter into the world in the work of creation and in the leading of history. The Word and the Holy Spirit are not means to safeguard the distance between God and the world, but exactly the opposite—they serve to avoid any such distance."[15]

Human beings are understood as created good in their totality; we are created in the image of God with Jesus Christ as the model. Christ was considered one of the descendants of Adam and Eve but was not overcome by the powers of evil. "What took place in the incarnation was that . . . the divine and the human were forever bound into one," writes Justo González, a historical theologian.[16]

Here, the finite is capable of the infinite. In fact, the very work of redemption effected by Christ was to restore the creation, to break the power of sin and evil, and to join the divine and the human as it had been intended at the creation. The sacraments, then, are expressions of grace themselves; the bread and wine become the body and blood of Jesus Christ.

There is obviously a higher valuation of the goodness of material life by this model; it is more sanguine about human bodies and the physical world. There tends to be less appreciation for the pervasiveness of sinfulness and less reliance on human reasoning. There is a much greater appreciation of the immanence of God and a sense that God's transcendence is somewhat impersonal. There is greater reliance upon the internal voice of revelation. When it comes to ethics, this model would tend to phrase questions in a way that would ask where God is present in the world, and to identify those activities that can be identified with God. Much greater emphasis is placed on discernment and the intuition of God's immanence; the heart as well as the head are seen as sources of revelation. This model is expressed in the theology of the Roman Catholic Church, and to some extent also in the Lutheran Church. The question we would ask of its theology and ethics of eating, then, is: "Where is God present in our eating, and how can we be about the redemptive work of God in our eating?"

While this has been only a brief summary of two incarnational models, it has the virtue of compressing many theological traditions into practical concerns. Both models can easily fit within the biblical tradition and both express major currents in the flow of Christian thought. In addition, they can be seen as complementary in the sense that the Alexandrine has the considerable advantage of fostering careful thought about the purposes and will of God in light of revelation, while the Antiochene is open to the insights of the visceral and material.

Toward a Theology of Eating

Having located the causes of our theological neglect of eating, we are now able to construct a feasible and engaging alternative. My proposed reconstruction has several benchmarks that I want to highlight clearly and bluntly. I want you to know my major conclusions so that you can focus on the argument by which we will get there.

Here is my bottom line: *Food is itself a means of revelation. Through eating together we taste the goodness of God.*

Here is my transformative revelation: *God intends food and eating to be for the purposes of delight and sharing.*

The remainder of this chapter will invite you to consider various models or ways of thinking about food that are in accord with the biblical themes we have excavated. We can think of these models as lenses or channels of revelation; they are ways of looking at the world.

BUILDING ON THE ANTIOCHENE MODEL

It seems all but axiomatic that we live in a world constructed on the base of a scientific/secular model aligned with the theistic mode of faith. In finding a model that would address the culture evangelistically, the church in the United States has often adopted an Alexandrine model that can too easily slide into theism. That is, because the transcendence of God is emphasized in the Alexandrine tradition, the presence of God appears remote from immediate experience. The divine can appear separated from the human, out of a concern that the two be seen as discrete natures. The discreteness of the nature of Christ can slide over into a separation of the world from God. God, in effect, ceases to be present if we human beings are not alert to God's presence. Food and eating can come to be seen as only functional and devoid of spiritual significance.

When we turn instead to the Antiochene model as a base, the claim is that God penetrates all life, that the realm of the human and finite is filled with the presence of God. In an age in which God appears merely optional, it is important for the community of faith to affirm the ongoing presence of God in all of life. In an age threatened by ecological degeneration, it is vital to claim that the Godhead is involved in all of nature and loves all that God has created. The incarnation of Jesus the Christ, the Antiochene model claims, affirms the ongoing involvement of God in the world. The world is suffused with the presence of God rather than being infused only occasionally. There is a strong emphasis on *perichoresis* here—the Spirit is the person of the Godhead who witnesses the penetration of all aspects of life. Usually *perichoresis* is defined as the "dance" of the life of the Trinity. Thus our concern is to point to locations and activities where God is especially present.[17] Food and eating are meaning-laden and relational.

This understanding is in happy conformity with our notion of "working theology" enunciated above. If theology is concerned not so much to get our doctrines right as to be the channel of transforming insights, then it is clearly intended to assist humankind in responding to God's activity in ways that will promote the health and well-being of all life in the cosmos. How can the body of Christ promote the optimum health of all life? In putting the question this way, we are appealing to the universal inclusiveness of Jesus the Christ at table—a basic and overwhelming biblical norm. We are also appealing to the goodness of the entire created order, not simply to the goodness of the human species, and not simply to the goodness and beauty of the whole for the sake of the human.

We are claiming that God is present in the world, affirming and active in all that makes for the good of the whole. It is a matter of faith, and one that we must wrestle with in the realms of policy analysis and lifestyle and world trade and nutrition and environmental science. It is also a matter of the values that we as individual Christians and as the corporate church wish to live out and promote. It is a matter of revelation for us and thus of insights that transform our lives, and that we wish to invite others to live out and enjoy.

Food as Revelation

Food itself is revelatory—and eating only more so. Adopting an Antiochene model, we claim that God is fully present in the earth, the plants and animals, human labor, and the beauty of all that is. "God pervades the world in the same way as honey in the comb," wrote Tertullian.[18] Eating is the most intimate, sensual act; it is how the world enters into us and how we become part of the world. This hunger, this appetite to eat, to taste the gift of love that comes to us from others and allow ourselves to be transformed by that love: this is revelation. We also share food with others; we give pleasure to others; and their delight likewise transforms us. Food is revelatory of the goodness and joy of the earth; it is also how we come to taste the language of grace and love; it is how we come to know community. Food opens up in us the visceral channels of knowledge. It enables us to experience love before we have a name for it. God comes to feed us, to fill us, to love us. We know grace first through our bodies.

We do not usually place the accent in revelation on the visceral. In part that is because the whole-body experience is impossible to reproduce in written form. As we contemplate how far short our writing falls from the whole experience, we may simply shake our heads and abandon the effort. But—in so doing—we leave the emphasis in revelation on the cognitive. We usually believe that because it is impossible to pass along the meaning of the experience cognitively, we have to settle for "third-level discourse," that is, merely talking about the experience (see references to Gadamer's thought in chapter 1). I think not. The meaning of the experience of food is precisely *in the experience itself,* in the eating. Thus revelation comes in eating. How can I tell you about the *cucinetta al pisella* at Tra Papuzzi on the Borgo Pio near the Vatican? You have to experience it.[19] Cooking and gardening are other practices that partake of and appreciate this form of revelation. They also mediate revelation.

One of my students—a farm wife from Illinois—has the right angle on food. She wrote, "Food is love. When food is used as God intended, it can manifest God's love for us as well as our response to that love. This love is of the first magnitude, no meager rations here, only the finest and the best—at no cost, freely given for all."[20]

How does one exposit the revelation of that which has to be experienced, of that which is known in the tasting and seeing and smelling and touching? I can appreciate why few have tried. Yet, the difficulties in conveying this revelation should not dissuade us from an interpretation of food and eating that is an alternative to mainstream culture's (and theology's) view of food as descriptive and functional. Theirs is a shallow view of food and eating and is entirely consonant with a scientific, rational view of human life abstracted from our ecological context.

By way of contrast, I claim an understanding of food and eating as meaning-laden, relational, and performative. This understanding is in essential continuity with the biblical directions we discovered in chapter 2 and is theologically promising.

Food Is Meaning-Laden

Food comes to our tables with an ecological history, with human effort, and with its own flavor. It can only be reduced to its functions through a failure to respect the "otherness" of food. Food has distinctive qualities, which it brings to our eating. To some extent food is a mystery to us.

Food and eating are meaning-laden. There are qualities and a history and—yes—functions that give food and eating meaning in themselves. We focus on food first. The spinach for my dinner salad grew in a particular soil in a particular topography in a particular climate; it was extracted from the soil and transported some distance by human means; it was then washed—or not—and sold either to a packaging facility or to a local grocer. And I want to buy prewashed spinach in cellophane to reduce my labor! This sort of preference is a pretty good example of a descriptive-functional view of food.

The spinach and its evolutionary history are another facet of its meaning. How growing occurs, how spinach nourishes the human being, and how people's tastes for spinach differ—all are mysteries whose scientific explanations only push the mystery back to a level we are satisfied not to explore further.

All these are aspects of spinach that we as human beings can easily ignore. However, to genuinely understand food as meaning-laden, we do well to fathom some of the dynamics, history, ecology, and human effort that go into food. The meaning of food is more than its capacity to be eaten by human beings, though it includes that.

Let me mention some of the qualities or meanings with which food confronts us when we are alert. Food, first of all, reminds us of our own physicality. Its physical nature stands over against us and, as we ingest it, that food becomes part of us. That which was grown in soil with the aid of sunlight and rain becomes us. Moreover, food resists our simply absorbing it; usually we have to buy, gather, grow, arrange, cook, present, and chew food. Eating is, in fact, a form of work that still offers resistance in a culture inclined to point and click.[21]

These meanings remind us of who we are, reflecting our own qualities. So food and eating remind us that (1) we are natural beings who are part of the ecological flow; (2) that we are limited beings who frequently run into those limits; (3) that we are dependent beings fed and nourished by soil; (4) that we may well enjoy forces that oppose easy co-option, such as growing and cooking; and (5) that there is a world of beings, objects, and forces out there beyond our own selves. That spinach or blackberry or fish may or may not be destined for human consumption; men and women likewise exist beyond easy "consumption" or co-optation by others. Well, that's a lot of meaning to attribute to spinach.

Food is revelatory in all these ways, many of which tie into a theological view of life. We are fed beyond ourselves by providential forces, only some of which we have to bend to our purposes. Many of them don't even have to be bent at all—wild blackberries or oranges in an old orchard or fresh water. What could testify more explicitly to the created goodness of the world, God's world, or to the providence of God who blessed us with abundance and continues to bless us? There are other biblical themes that food and eating open unto us. There is the *eucharista* that is generated by eating a ripe peach or a lamb chop; there is gratitude and appreciation for all that generates delight. There is also a pre-cruciform revelation of the sacrifice that creation makes for our well-being. Indeed, we are fed beyond our knowledge and certainly beyond our desserts. Food and eating witness to the grace of God, a grace that we first know in our taste buds and sucking lips and satisfied stomachs. Who could believe otherwise than that God creates food and eating for delight?

Furthermore, if indeed "the world is more beautiful than it is useful,"22 we are confronted—nay, struck down—by the beauty of kiwis, apples, bananas, artichokes, broccoli, carrots, and peaches. The beauty of fields of wheat and sunflowers and pecan orchards and gigantic stalks of corn—all are more beautiful than they need to be. They manifest the beauty of God. They awaken us to the sensibility of the world; they call us to an appreciation of all that is.

Food Is Relational

Food and eating are also relational. We have already seen how primordially relational eating is; the baby suckling at her mother's breast knows that pretty well. Eating itself is something most people like to do with others. It is a basic social act. Because food is relational, it ties us into the whole world beyond ourselves. Eating connects us with others, whether we are alert to this connection or not. We depend on many others to grow our food in ways that are both healthy and safe. This is not only a human-to-human relationship; it is a human-to-other-species relationship. There is also a close connection with the land itself and the species that make up soil, with businesspeople, with farmers and rural communities, and with our eating companions. The amount of fossil energy, soil energy, and human energy that goes into the production of food connects us to a vast web of others. Simple reflection on the act of eating food will reveal that a host of others are present with us at table.

The fact of eating also indicates to us that we are ourselves embodied beings. It is clear that we eat when hungry or restless or whatever, and that what we eat nourishes and sustains us. Eating reveals that we are embodied. Our diet and access to foods show that we are located in particular places and that our thought and action themselves are contingent on the particularity of our embodied locatedness. An awareness of the particularity of our social location is essential for an accurate self-awareness and an awareness of others. Our embodied relation to nature derives from the fact that we eat nature. We are sustained by nature and we sustain nature, or not.

The embodiment that eating and food reveal also underscores the apodictic nature of our relation to others who are likewise embodied.[23] We share embodiment with others; we are related to others through the food we eat. The manner in which we eat with others generates relationship and reinforces relation. The fact of eating also entails a sensuality that awakens our senses in addition to taste and smell. Thus food is often associated with sexuality, as shown in films such as *Like Water for Chocolate, Woman on Top, Chocolat*, and *Big Night* suggest.

Delight shared is doubly enjoyable. Food and eating indicate another way that we are essentially relational beings—through our senses. Why we should take such delight in sharing food with others is finally a mystery but very much a fact of our nature. God created us and blessed us with sociality. We enjoy table fellowship with other people; many of us hate to eat alone and will read or watch television or otherwise distract ourselves when we do eat by ourselves.

Being hospitable to others gives us pleasure; food is one way we express affection for others. It is a vehicle and a generator of hospitality and community. It is one of God's ways of fostering relationship, of increasing our delight. Appreciation of food and eating are a response to the blessing and delight of food, an appreciation that increases with our mindfulness of food. We appreciate others and we want to become intimate with them; one way that God does that, and we do so in imitation, is by feasting together.

To some extent we choose our eating companions and the places and diet we enjoy. To a greater extent the processes involved in eating are involuntary just like so many bodily processes. There is a mysterious component to the way that food establishes and is a product of relationality. Food and eating reveal that we human beings are strangers to ourselves; we do not know the involuntary processes that are integral to our lives. Likewise, food and eating reveal the strange graciousness and approachability of others who are remarkably trustworthy. We can sense that we have been graced from beyond ourselves and also within ourselves. Relationality is good beyond our choices about whom we associate or eat with.

The gift of food and eating, the delight we enjoy in eating together, the strange blessedness of sharing—all point toward an appreciation that begs to be shared. This sense of enjoyment is expansive; we feel so good that we want others to feel the same. One reason why we contribute to relieving world hunger is our empathy—the drive to share goodness. Another is our sympathy—the desire to assist others in avoiding the pain of real hunger. These deep forces push us to act in ways that are compassionate and just. These avenues satisfy a deep craving in us to express the grace of the relationships through which God has graced us. Christians affirm that the way of the cross is finally the way to gain one's life, to live fully and abundantly. Food and eating remind us that we are here not only to delight, but also to share.

Food Is Performative

Food, we have said, is meaning-laden and relational. It is also performative. A word is performative when it implies an action; indeed, the word itself indicates an action. One clear example is that of promising: to promise something is to bind oneself to perform the thing promised. All vows are performative. Words imply that we will act in a way that is in agreement with them; we try to "keep our word." I believe that certain actions are also performative. By engaging in them we commit (or tend to commit) ourselves toward acting in certain related or implied ways. There is usually a tendency to continue to act in certain ways in certain situations. This may be the basis of habits and virtues. We may speak of virtues, then, as having a performative character. My point here, however, is not that broad; rather, I want to suggest that eating has a performative character for Christians.

The biblical and theological tradition we have described points in the direction of certain responses (or performatives) to the created goodness and blessing of food, to the providence it exemplifies, and to the hospitality it expresses toward us. Food is a gift; eating is a blessing. We say grace in recognition of the giftedness of the way food comes to our table. In a real way, food is gratuitous. It is not something we can claim to have a right to by dint of anything we are or can do. The monetary price of food is no compensation for the miraculous gift of soil or the conscientious work of the laborers whose efforts enable us to buy it, much less the conjunction of the natural miracles that grow the plant or animal. Food and eating retain a residual edge of being gifts to us. We respond to gifts in gratitude and by passing along the gift. The goodness of food so fills us that it overflows and pushes us to share that goodness. For the Christian, this amounts to a performative edge in eating. Furthermore, this performative edge implies a sharing that is itself a delight.

The performative element of responding to God's goodness depends on being sensitive to and recognizing the rich meaning of food. When eating remains merely functional and descriptive, it loses this richness and its performative edge is dulled. There is a message here for the church: redefine eating and reclaim the meaning of food.

Christians also find that their appreciation of the meaning of food itself adds flavor to the way we savor food. We take great delight in eating because we know that God created food as a gracious delight for us. One can only assume that other species find enjoyment if not delight in their food as well. Our dog, Sparky, certainly seems to delight in lamb bones and doggie treats.

Jesus expressed gratuitousness in his inclusive table fellowship. The table of blessing is for all, those who can pay and those who cannot. Having graciously received, we are to perform grace for others. Our responses are ones of being hospitable to others, showing compassion, and working for justice so that all can enjoy eating and the other good things in this life. We respond to our world as stewards of sustainability so that the earth, other species, and all people can continue to delight.

There is, to be sure, often a discontinuity between our enjoyment and our sharing. We have to learn that sharing can sharpen our delight. There is an element of growth, of effort, in the process of sanctification. By calling eating performative, I do not mean to imply an automatic response but a visceral inclination acquired by deliberate and reflective effort. Striving to act in holy ways, in ways that reflect God's goodness and righteousness, entails conflict with our own selfishness and with cultural impulses.

Theologian Serene Jones builds on Calvin's view of sanctification by suggesting that one image of sanctification is performative. She sees grace moving in the Christian life and in such practices as eating in a formative way. "When we perform and are performed by grace, our lives take on the form that we are."[24]

Partaking of the Lord's Supper, Eucharist, is itself very much a performative act. By eating the body and drinking the blood of Jesus the Christ, we express our loyalty and dependence on Father, Son, and Spirit. We express our gratitude to God for all the goodness that comes from God's gracious incarnation, creation, and continuing presence. If that eating and drinking were more whole-bodied—if we were genuinely to eat a meal—then the thick layers of meaning in the ritual would not be so compressed. We could taste the delight of God's body being broken for us at the crucifixion and of our destruction being lifted. We do really celebrate that we who are "not worthy to receive God" are healed by God's Word and action.

At the table we do get a sense of union with others who are fellow believers, who link their destinies to the life, death, and resurrection of the Lord Jesus. The Eucharist expresses a dependency on God's goodness as we partake of daily bread and drink. Eating and drinking together create community.

Linking our loyalty and our fortunes with Jesus entails a commitment to discipleship, to carrying out the mission of Jesus. This specific eating and drinking is a way of expressing the sort of eating and drinking we will do when we come away from the Lord's table. We will share and we will delight, delight and share. We commit ourselves to include all others in table fellowship; we will proclaim God's love that we have experienced in this bread and wine by working for justice so that all will have enough to eat.

The Eucharist calls us to remember that God pervades the world, that grace is ultimately the force driving the world. The eating of the Supper of the Lord reveals the alternative reality that we too often lose sight of because we do not experience it. If we are to believe that God is immanent throughout the universe, then the church will have to incarnate the Eucharist in its life. One way of doing this is to relearn how to feast in appreciation of God's goodness—that is delight. The other is to share the feast in mission—to proclaim the goodness of God in effecting our redemption and the redemption of the world. The Eucharist is finally the feast of the world's redemption; that is performative with a vengeance. We who share Eucharist are to share the story of redemption and to live out the redeemed life.

EARLY IN THIS CHAPTER I claimed that food and eating were revelatory and that the twin purposes for which God intended food and eating were delight and sharing. The three guideposts—that food and eating are meaning-laden, relational, and performative—lay out the content of the revelation. In the course of developing this chapter, I have tested the twin purposes of delight and sharing. These two purposes comprise much of what the Christian tradition has understood as God's design in creation and redemption. They express the covenants that God has established with humankind. They are also sensitive to both the visceral element in knowledge and motivation (delight) and to the cognitive-reflective (sharing).

We have also explored two sources of criteria for judging whether our experience is Christian—Scripture and tradition—and have located some benchmarks to help us think. In the next several chapters, we explore the empirical and social contingencies that surround eating and the global food system, all the while continuing to develop our theology of eating as we also raise questions of morality. If a central purpose of theology is to help people live morally, then there is not a strict delineation between theology and ethics. We will be engaged in a reflective dialogue whereby experience tests our theology and ethics and assists in their further development, while our theological stance likewise seeks to elucidate and guide experience. The next chapters are less theoretical but not uncritically so. I adopt this stance because it is appropriate to a dynamic Antiochene theology. It allows me to make claims that are appropriate for relative absolutes. This is a working theology and ethics, and it will develop in conversation with the realities that accompany food, eating, and the food system.

Part Two

Eating and
Food System Disorders

God and Eating Disorders

For every one affluent white anorexic you create by "over-emphasizing" obesity, you create ten obese poor girls by downplaying the severity of the issue. . . . The number of kids with eating disorders is positively dwarfed by the numbers with obesity. It sidesteps the whole class issue. We've got to stop that and get on with the real problem. . . .

After controlling for smoking, the risk of death . . . increased by two percent for each pound of excess weight for ages 50 to 62, and by one percent per extra pound for ages 30 to 49.

—Greg Critser, *Fat Land*

"EXPERTS SAY We're Getting Fat," blares the Newscape/Associated Press release. How many times have you read a similar story? Seems as though more people across the entire world are becoming more obese. Fifteen percent of China's adult population is overweight, reports the Worldwatch Institute. The usual culprits are cited: not enough exercise, fast food, the pace of modern life, automobile culture, poor sidewalks, and the list goes on.

I can tell you about fat.

Fat is standing in line waiting to be chosen for a kickball game and everyone else, everyone, is chosen before you are. As the names are called out, you just pray that yours will not be the last. Even little girls are chosen before you, even though you are male and stand taller (and weigh more) than anyone in your grade.

Fat is deciding not to participate in sports anymore. It is cajoling your parents to ask the principal to permit you not to play kickball or soccer or volleyball or whatever. Fat is sitting and reading, and reading and sitting, and eating and eating and eating.

Fat is being conscious of how much space you take up. It is being aware that others are looking at you and resenting the fact that they have to crowd together because of you.

Fat is going to the refrigerator on an exploratory jaunt every time you are restless or not totally engaged in what you are doing.

Fat is having been so big for so long that even when someone tells you that you look slim now, you don't believe them.

I know fat. I was one of those many people in the world who struggle with being fat, and I battle with overeating all the time.

All of this got connected with God in my mind. I remember praying fervently that God would let me do pull-ups so that I could get my physical fitness merit badge to advance to the Eagle Scout rank.

I remember thinking about how God considers fatness. Did Jesus have a weight problem? None of the pictures I saw even vaguely hinted at that. Jesus was always slim and trim. Did God like fat people? Would the Holy Spirit work through fat people? Why did God make me want to eat all the time?

Heavy theological questions, huh?

Somehow I did get the message that God loved everyone, including even fat people—even people who ate compulsively, or who got chosen last for kickball. Getting that message was a salvific moment, a revelation.

My personal experience is what interests me so much about food and God now, and it has led me to many important questions. What is eating? How is God involved in the wonderful world of food? What does the incarnation of Jesus Christ have to say about food and eating? In what sorts of eating practices did Jesus engage? How is the Holy Spirit involved in the ongoing world of eating and the way food gets distributed?

The seed of this book was in me when I was in fifth grade, waiting in line to be picked for a kickball game. And eating is still a very personal and a very religious question for me.

Two other items from the news report caught my attention: Data from the United Nations (UN) agency, WHO (World Health Organization), indicate that at least 1.1 billion people worldwide get too few calories to ward off hunger, while another 1.1 billion or more of us take in too many. Even those in the middle group often lack enough vitamins and minerals.

It's easy to predict, asserts Barry Popkin, a nutrition professor at the University of North Carolina, that many countries will wind up looking like the United States, where fully half of its citizens are overweight and inactive.[1]

Positive and Negative Hunger

The models for food and eating expressed in Scripture and much of the theological tradition point to God's twin purposes for eating: delight and sharing. To be sure, both of these are predicated on the availability of sufficient food of good quality that people can actually delight in and share.

So far, we have more or less been viewing hunger as a desire that is positive and promotes health—a bodily desire that is natural, enjoyable, and encouraging of other values. Hunger, real hunger, is also disordered and disordering. In its extreme form, of course, it destroys even the possibility of other values and certainly contravenes the values of delight and sharing.

It is hard to avoid the subject of eating disorders. Our cultural usage has tended to limit that phrase to such disorders as bulimia and anorexia and obesity. That is itself an interesting limitation because of what it distorts. For one thing, the two disorders that are most explicitly included—bulimia and anorexia—tend to be associated with women, so we think of this as a women's problem. For another, all three disorders *can* be seen as merely individual. The book *Fat Land,* however, makes a strong case that obesity is a national and corporately sponsored problem that has been consciously engineered.

We are broadening the category of eating disorder here to include all that diverges from a healthy order of eating. Thus we are adopting a focus that is social, ecological, and economic as well as individual, consumerist, and lifestyle-oriented.

According to the United Nations, "more people die from malnutrition and starvation each year than die from all natural disasters combined?"[2] That sure sounds like a real global disorder, not just one person's personal battle with overeating!

Is there a religious implication here? The Christian church's organized fight against world hunger is well established—CROP walks, for example. Concern about world hunger grows out of the conviction that God cares for hungry people, and that Christians should follow Christ's example of compassion for those who are hungry. But what other implications might there be? How does the gospel relate to those who are overweight or eating unwisely? Are eating disorders "sinful"?

This chapter begins by projecting several different types of disorder—systemic, lifestyle, interpersonal, and personal. It then moves to the Christian question of how sin is involved in disorder. Finally, it asks whether there is redemption for eating disorders.

Types of Eating Disorders

To avoid inducing immobilizing guilt and to deal candidly with our eating problems, let me adapt the concept of the "hungry ghost" from the Tibetan Book of the Dead. The realm of the hungry ghost is that of disordered desire, possession, and hunger. The hungry ghost images someone with an eating disorder. Possessed of an enormous stomach, slender neck, and tiny mouth, hungry ghosts never get enough of what they desire. They can never fill the hunger in their huge stomachs. Even after eating all day long, they still crave food. There is no joy in eating, just the pain of having to satisfy their deprivations. Clearly the food that hungry ghosts crave is seldom directed *only* at meeting nutritional needs; eating obsessively is a way of meeting other needs as well.[3] Sometimes, I confess, we don't know who or what the hungry ghosts are. In my case, sometimes they are feeling hurt or envious or maybe just greedy. Food is a means of filling up whatever we sense we need. It is not just substitutionary; we turn to food because it does have some capacity to satisfy us. Nevertheless, it is only *linked* to what we most deeply crave. All of us who battle eating disorders are dealing with hungry ghosts.

SYSTEMIC OR GLOBAL DISORDER

It is vital to recognize that "hungry ghosts" are created by the same profit-driven global food system that promotes eating disorders as simply a personal problem. The system has encouraged us to internalize and individualize eating disorders as our own personal hungry ghosts and substitute eating for a myriad of other concerns. This is not incidental; it supports the continued growth of the system—and, not so incidentally, of ourselves. Christians have a stake in dealing with what has become a religion of eating and, in fact, consumption in general. Make no mistake: consumption is a religion that promises salvation and that many Americans—and many Christians—have bought into. But Christianity affirms that consuming does not save us. Ours is a story of salvation through faith and through the response to God of neighborliness.

When telling people about this project, I have often noticed very uncomfortable reactions among those who are overweight or have other eating disorders. I believe this stems from their negative feelings about their own weight problems and their belief that this is primarily a character deficiency for which they alone are responsible. My word to them—and to myself—is that eating disorders constitute a problem, a systemic as well as a personal problem, and that it is time for all of us to feel bad about the system that is destroying us as individuals and other peoples and species around the globe. This problem is also going to impact our children and grandchildren. There is no salvation to be found in this system. Its sin would continue even if we individually were to "slim down."

Of first importance, then, is recognition of *systemic* or *global food disorder* as the first and most problematic of four categories of disorder. It is a disorder of maldistribution that pervades the globe and fosters the sin of human starvation and species obliteration. This disorder also, in a different way, blinds us to our own (affluent nations') complicity in this sin and the way in which our own food disorders, especially obesity, are tied into systemic disorder. This disorder will receive some initial treatment here but is so significant that it will occupy its own, later chapter.

This first level of disorder is abetted by the second, that of *lifestyle disorders*, which distort the meaning of health and well-being. There is at least a modicum of complicity here for all who live in a system that promotes consumptive lifestyles that deliver comfort at the expense of others' survival. Third is *interpersonal, or family, disorder*, which arises in families and is the result of disordered family relations. Many family therapists have investigated the strong positive relationship between dysfunctional families and eating disorders. At the fourth level, there is the set of disorders that many see as the first level and which are often experienced as *personal disorders*. That is certainly the way I experienced (and often still experience) mine.

At the systemic level there is a structured and carefully orchestrated effort to foster distorted desire or concupiscence, not for itself but because it encourages consumer spending, corporate growth, and profitability. The values that dominate the food system are designed to promote a level of consumption and greed that will produce the greatest amount of profit and market share. Rather than design a system that will provide food for everyone (which is manifestly possible) and will delight all, the system is designed to produce food that is upscale, convenient, processed, and cheap for the consumers who can afford it. Little attention is paid to the health concerns of the buyer and even less attention to all those who cannot buy. Health, delight, survival, and sharing are not the values that predominate. A concern for health is secondary to that of making a profit, becoming prominent only when that is in the monetary best interest of the corporate member of the food system. Values are distorted to serve monetary gain. This systemic or global level of disorder affects all human beings; it distorts our desires and our reasoning ability.

In her book, *Starving for Salvation*, Michelle Lelwica sums up some of the dynamics that generate this global distortion for women in affluent countries. After explaining that "rationalism and enchantment are not mutually exclusive," she says:

> On the contrary, the present-day hegemony of consumer capitalism—an economic system owned and oriented by the commercial profit of a privileged few—thrives on its promises to alter reality, to alleviate pain, and to give "ultimate satisfaction." Like patriarchal religion, this imaginative system of material values feeds on the very dreams it functions to deter: dreams of freedom, equality, abundance. But in this technosymbolic universe of meaning, "ultimate values" are created and circulated through material consumer commodities, relationships are negotiated through monetary currency, freedom is sought through perpetual consumption, and reality is apprehended through glossy surfaces.[4]

If what Lelwica says is only half true, it confirms many of the dynamics we have associated with systemic disorder.

LIFESTYLE DISTORTIONS

The food industry spends billions of dollars each year on advertising and promotion to create an environment that constantly pressures us to consume. This is one linkage between the global systemic disorder evident in the food supply structure and how that disorder finds its way into the lifestyles of a particular culture. Perhaps it is not too much to claim that the food industry itself creates or nourishes the "hungry ghosts" of cultural values that foster disorders. (How much do we assume that "you can never be too rich or too thin"?) We will concentrate on the United States, but almost any industrialized "First World" nation would exhibit similar dynamics. While the food industry is partly to blame, it remains clear that the industry is responding to pressure from consumers; the food industry is both shaped by and shaping food and eating preferences.

I find it fascinating that scientists have no clear delineation between those who are classified as having an eating disorder and those who do not. Dr. Timothy Walsh, director of the eating disorders research program at New York State Psychiatric Institute in Manhattan says, "While we have made progress, we have also recognized how much we don't know, even about who should be considered as having an eating disorder."[5] This reinforces the perspective that there is a systemic or global disorder that translates into a lifestyle or cultural disorder and into interpersonal and personal disorders.

Further extending this perspective is Dr. Kelly Brownell's view that "Americans are exposed to a toxic food environment. The word 'toxic' is not too strong. There are dangerous agents in the [nutritional] environment that are widely available and that cause people to be sick."[6] Americans have almost immediate access to a poor diet—to high-calorie foods that are inexpensive, widely available, heavily promoted, and good tasting. These ingredients, according to Dr. Brownell, "produce a predictable, understandable, and inevitable consequence—an epidemic of diet-related diseases."[7]

The rise in the percentage of people who are obese and overweight has been attributed not only to what we eat but also to how infrequently we exercise. Our sedentary lifestyle (complete with remote control, Internet, and computer outreach and games) is blamed for our lack of exercise.

There are two other factors in our lifestyle that contribute to eating distortions: one is our cultural values; the second has to do with how we eat with others. We turn first to values. There are—and this is very significant—contradictory impulses in our culture: one is a desire to devour everything and the other a longing to subsist on spirit alone with a perfect body. Between the two, "millions of people with undiagnosed or 'sub-clinical' versions of eating disorders pass for normal in a culture where 'normal' is becoming weirder and more contradictory all the time," writes Dr. Mary Sykes Wylie.[8]

Furthermore, in a culture that equates thin with good and fat with bad, even though the percentage of us who are overweight is rising, the self-control and discipline that the anorexic person exemplifies signifies a triumph of the spirit over the will.[9]

A final evidence of disorder in our lifestyles has to do with how we eat with others—or do not. Often it seems as though efficiency and speed in eating has replaced the fun of eating with others. Food eaten alone and quickly may be experienced as a kick or a rush or even as a comfort, but loses its joy as a social act and as a frame for togetherness. Wylie suggests that we shouldn't blame social forces alone for this, but she does claim:

It's hard to imagine a society more conducive to disordered patterns of eating, however defined, than ours. For the first time in history, not only has it become normal and usual to eat alone, and easy to get food with no work at all, but much of the industrialized, mass-produced food culture—fast-food drive-in windows, take-out delis, shopping-mall food courts, prepackaged "single servings" sold in supermarkets—seem created specifically for the lonely, non-cooking muncher eating in front of the television, feeling depressed and unworthy, watching Calvin Klein models cavorting on the screen.[10]

INTERPERSONAL DISORDERS

"Our food habits have become increasingly desocialized, fragmented, evolutionarily primitive," says Richard Gordon, a therapist specializing in eating disorders. "In the typical American household, the average number of dinners eaten together is three per week, with the average length of dinner being 20 minutes."[11] Another therapist even reported that for a certain percentage of patients, eating face-to-face with another person, without the distraction of television or some other activity, was perceived as so risky that she had to prescribe very small steps toward engaging in such an activity.

It occurs to me that this may not seem very disordered, perhaps not deserving of the notion of being a disorder at all. However, if the fear is of relating to another person, which is precisely what appears to be the case, then we are in the realm of disorder. Food is a substitute for the real "hungry ghost," which is deprivation of interpersonal relationships and knowing how to relate to others.

Male and female body images have much to do with whether someone feels worthy of an interpersonal relationship, whether one has sufficient self-esteem to attempt relating to others. The way that adolescent and younger girls, and increasingly boys of the same age, feel about their bodies has everything to do with how they approach others and eating. Two recent books detail just how painful it can be to have a negative body image, no matter the reality of the person's body.[12] In a culture where the average woman is 5'4" and weighs 144 pounds and the average female model is 5'10" and weighs 111 pounds, there is real dissonance between the actual and the ideal. For adolescent boys, bulking up and being able to take care of oneself is an analogous obsession. When these two average people begin to relate to one another, the ideal woman and the ideal man may also be present as images and may be perceived as standing in judgment of the actual.

The point is that interpersonal relationships are difficult, and often it is easier to eat alone than to face the threat of relating. Food and eating become part of the disorder rather than being an enjoyable addition to and generator of relationship.

But eating alone is simply a symptom of the disorder. The real disorder is that we have abrogated responsibility for each other and, at the most tangible level, responsibility for caring for each other physically and materially. We believe that "it's my own business if I eat alone." We experience no feelings of complicity in the hunger of peoples worldwide, who are part of our brothers and sisters in God's family.

PERSONAL DISORDERS

It is this level of extreme disorder that is usually meant when a therapist or journalist refers to "eating disorders." Often it refers to only bulimia (binging and purging) or anorexia (starving oneself), but sometimes includes obesity as well. In this section, we refer to all three but should note that personal disorders are a consequence of forces operating on the other three levels as well—the systemic or global, the lifestyle or cultural, and the interpersonal. One gets a very different perspective on eating disorders by setting them in a broader frame of reference. For one thing, this avoids part of the "just world" hypothesis, which renders all individuals responsible for whatever they are or do. This broader setting enables us to see that there are many factors besides personal history and accountability that explain why a person is bulimic or obese.[13]

Michelle Lelwica has performed a great service by gathering the various theories about what contributes to bulimia and anorexia.[14] She rehearses the relevant psychological, medical, and sociocultural/feminist theories, but then synthesizes them into a religious and ethical theory. She claims that girls and women starve, binge, and purge their bodies as a means of coping with the pain and injustice of their daily lives. Showing how our contemporary culture produces feelings of emptiness and dissatisfaction in girls and women, Lelwica argues that society ignores and denies their spiritual needs. One way that girls and women deal with this is to construct a network of symbols, beliefs, and rituals around food and their bodies. I suspect that, had she expanded her considerations to obesity, she could easily have established that a similar sort of pattern operates for boys and men.

What emerges is a popular salvation myth that encourages girls and women to fixate on their bodies and engage in disordered eating patterns. The male equivalents are bodybuilding and obsessive eating. While this myth provides a sense of meaning and purpose in the face of uncertainty and injustice, such rigid and unhealthy devotion to the body only deepens the spiritual void that women yearn to fill. The consequences of this longing for salvation are extreme. Many girls and women literally starve to death in this way each year, and those who live suffer serious health effects. According to Dr. Jane Brody, "Short of death from heart failure, chronic starvation can cause severe osteoporosis, dangerously low blood pressure and damage to the kidneys and liver."[15]

There is an obsessive, desperate quality to the first-person accounts of eating disorders that I have read. Furthermore, when I typed "eating disorders" into my search engine, I found literally thousands of websites, many of which offered to help others overcome their disorders as the authors of those sites had done. Throughout these accounts there runs a thread—actually it is more like a rope—that characterizes virtually each of the victims of disorder: an intense longing for connection with other people. In literally no case did any victims of eating disorders feel a strong sense of community with others; in many cases, women attribute their success at overcoming the hell of eating disorders to the loving relationship of someone who would not give up on them.

A composite portrait of eating disorders emerges—a sense of isolation from others, an individual grasping that is anything but contentedly enjoying the results of such grasping, an addictive quality. The hungry ghosts of this disorder are ravenous. My image is that they are grasping almost anything that promises to alleviate the yearning for something, anything, to fill them up. The sensation is akin to panic or not being fully cognizant of what one is doing. Striving to control these impulses, the person seeks a fix in any place where they have experienced satisfaction.

This disorder, it has become obvious, is about desire, about hunger. It is one way in which the search for wholeness takes place. The most astonishing account I read, Margaret Bullitt-Jonas's *Holy Hunger*, is subtitled "A Memoir of Desire."[16] In it Bullitt-Jonas speaks of compulsive eating as "thoroughly nonsensual." For her it was a craving, a greed, a compulsion, but never something she loved. "I would have loved to have loved it," she writes.[17] Instead, for her it had "very little to do with providing fuel for my body, with giving myself pleasure, or with opening my heart to love. It had everything to do with desperately trying to communicate. . . . All I was giving myself was food, when what I really hungered for was embodied love."[18] At base, eating disorders are a case of distorted substitutionary desire, of searching for love in food, of seeking love and salvation in oneself, without relationship.

Eating Disorders and the Doctrine of Sin

At this point we relate the doctrine of sin to the several levels of disorder that we have described. The purpose in doing this is not to pass judgment or to condemn, but to render a more incisive analysis so that we can transform our habits and social order. The doctrine of sin, especially in this case, can help us understand why we become disordered and how we can redirect our desires and lives toward a healthier order of living. The Christian understanding of sin is a diagnosis that also serves as a prescription for health. The point is not judgment, but discernment and rehabilitation toward a restoration of God's order.

We have seen that the disorders we have chronicled drive out delight and sharing. They eventuate in vastly different realities than enjoyment and fellowship and neighborliness. Instead, they produce lives that are at best limited and contorted, perhaps isolated and isolating, even painful and destructive. At worst they result in starvation, whether that death is of a Congolese baby caught in the vortex of war-induced agricultural famine or of an American college coed who has suffered fatal heart failure.

Eating disorders are the result of distorted desires for wholeness and salvation that cannot be fulfilled short of God's grace. They are painful as sin itself, and there is seldom, if ever, joy in sin. They are hungry ghosts who can never be filled, but whose craving and grasping and self-conscious emptiness violate our happiness and put us on the treadmill of concupiscence. Following God's desires, discerning God's activity, and partnering with God's action in the world—however expressed—are the ways to fulfillment. These are the ways to enjoy our lives to the fullest, as we were created to do.

Sin destroys that enjoyment.[19] Thomas Aquinas, whose thought both Luther and Calvin appreciated, proposed useful division of sin. Aquinas reasoned "on the one hand" that "we can divide sin into three domains of disordered acts: (1) gluttony and lust and similar sins against oneself, (2) thievery and murder and similar forms of injustice against one's neighbor, and (3) lack of faith or hope and similar sins against God. Yet, on the other hand, because the divine order includes the orders of self and society, there is a sense in which we can say all sins are against God."[20]

Aquinas's classification of gluttony and greed as sins against the self is a useful way to begin analyzing eating disorders. Such eating disorders are sins against the self, which result in considerable pain for the self. We will consider here the individual level of disorder first.

The cumulative development of sin helps us to understand better the personal level of eating disorders. Theologian Ted Peters, for example, proposes that there are seven steps toward radical evil or sin.[21]According to Peters, evil begins, as does sin, with the dynamic of anxiety.[22] The fact that men and women experience anxiety is not itself sinful, but it can lead us to sin.

We fall into sin with the second stage, that of distrust. We distrust that God (or others) will care for us, and our anxiety is thereby increased and we begin to think that we need to take care of ourselves.[23] For eating disorders this stage may take the form of feeling as though we can never "be enough" or "do enough" or merit the love of others. There is no hope; we begin to feel the gnawing of those hungry ghosts.

The third stage is pride, treating ourselves as God. This is evident in those of us who almost unconsciously consume more than our share of the earth's resources. Pride may engender the most pernicious sort of sin—the sense of entitlement. We who over-consume habitually may become disconnected from others, from self, and from God through our hubris.

Thus far our account of sin has followed Peters's, but we need to supplement his account by recognizing a second form of sin: self-contempt. For those of us with eating disorders, this third stage may not take the form of hubris as much as it does the despair that comes from feeling unloved. Self-contempt arises out of a despair born of underestimation of our abilities and inherent goodness, and it seems to be rooted in self-negation rather than pride.

The fourth stage of this sequence is concupiscence, which is identified as coterminous with sensuality, the desire to possess, the hunger to acquire, consumerism, lust, covetousness, and greed. The eating disorders of selfish consumption and the need to have more and more as a substitute for other goods is easily understood with the terms *gluttony* and *greed*. This is the sin of violating one's own body and selfhood, but the nature of the sin is wanting more than one's share, treating one's own desires and needs as more important than those of others.

Concupiscence illuminates another form of sin that arises from self-loathing: the sense of not being enough. The disorders of bulimia, anorexia, and obesity may be born of distorted desire. In this case, the eating disorder is misnamed if we simply accept it as "gluttony." To the person who loathes herself or himself, all desires or hungers may seem illegitimate. She or he may feel unworthy of having any desires fulfilled. She or he may see all such desires as concupiscence. In this case, the eating disorder is misnamed if we accept it as simply "gluttony."[24]

The next stage Peters describes is self-justification, which involves a denial of one's own sinfulness and a rejection of the need for grace. I believe that this is the route of gluttony as conventionally understood and of the social sin of over-consumption. Eating disorders born of underestimation, however, exhibit an opposite difficulty: a crushing sense of one's own sinfulness and a sense that there could never be enough grace for personal redemption. This is anything but self-justification; it is a denial of the possibility of acceptance and justification.

The sixth stage, for those who manifest self-justification, is that of cruelty, a lack of empathy with others, and a conscious and direct infliction of pain on them. This stage also exhibits insensitivity and a lack of self-critical distance. For those who deny the possibility of justification, the next stage might well be despair, a crushing sensitivity to the judgment of others as reinforcing one's own condemnatory judgment.

These sins take on an opposite but mirror image at the third stage. That is, the nature of the guilt they evidence is related to the same issue but moves in opposite directions. My own sense is that gluttony is a sin to which we become insensitive through complicity—a complicity that knows we stand to benefit from such gluttonous policies as cheap food, export subsidies, market penetration, and exploitation of the poor.

Peters's final stage is that of blasphemy against God—radical evil that is both overt and covert. It is evil as a subversion of the divine symbols. Perhaps failing to appreciate God's good gifts, such as food, borders on blasphemy. I find this stage less illuminative for our purposes than Peters's other stages, and thus will not elaborate.

What has become quite clear through experimenting with these stages is that there are two types of sin: one is characterized by gluttony, greed, and desensitized over-consumption; the other is characterized by the sin of negative self-assessment or self-loathing. Feminists have made this point, but tracing eating disorders through these stages has brought home to me the experiential reality of this form of sinful eating disorder. This is not, I say assuredly, exclusively a female disorder. And it is very important to recognize that not all sin is born of pride, as are gluttony and greed.

THE UNDERSIDE OF GLUTTONY

If we identify all eating disorders with the deadly sin of gluttony, I believe that we miss a profound dimension of sin. Not only that, but we run the risks of misdiagnosing a self-esteem disorder and of judgmentalism. Furthermore, if the source of sin is a basic underestimation of who we are, then talk of grabbing for too much, consuming too much, will not quench the hunger that generates this disorder. To be sure, gluttony is a sin that we are socialized, perhaps even forced, to participate in. However, imagine that you are starved for genuine human caring and eat obsessively in order to compensate for a gnawing fear that you will never be good enough or acceptable enough. Imagine then reading: "Concupiscence creates the illusion that having constitutes being, that consuming can combat anxiety. . . . At the heart of concupiscence is the denial of our own limits expressed through the consumption of someone else's life-giving power."[25]

To be sure, there are numerous ways that social gluttony feeds into sin. However, for the person who feels all too desperately the reality of her or his limits, and who wishes simply to "be" enough for oneself and others, this understanding of concupiscence not only misses the mark but comes across as judgmental. There is no doubt that in too much consumption there is real concupiscence.On the other hand, there is also real legitimate desire in consumption for the good things that God has given us. It is not desire that is sin, nor is it the anxiety that leads to sin; it is seeking the ultimate in the penultimate and mistaking food for salvation and eating for God. Aquinas got it right: gluttony is a sin against the self, but the source of that sin is not only over-reaching or grasping, it can also be under-reaching and fear of one's unworthiness.

ADDICTION

There is a body of literature that links eating disorders born of self-loathing or under-esteem to addiction. Bullitt-Jonas does this at several points.[26] This is a helpful linkage for understanding the experience of eating disorder as an obsession over which one can feel powerless. This linkage makes sense of the divergent qualities of sin discussed above. There is much to be learned from the association of self-loathing and under-esteem with addiction, but that must merely be acknowledged here.

One common notion about addiction, however, must be resisted. That is the inference that one is not at all complicit in one's addiction or in any sense culpable. Indeed, however mysterious the seductive force of the addiction, we are to some extent accountable for having entered into it. I would not underestimate the difficulty of struggling out of addiction (particularly as a former cigarette smoker), but neither would I discount God's power to redeem us from our addictions. In fact, Christians are called to mediate that redemptive grace as efficaciously and intelligently as we can. We need to enter into the contradictions and the mysterious complicity of addictions, and we can best do that by seeking an analysis that is as insightful as possible.

I do not wish too quickly to reconnect the divergent nature of eating disorders lest we fail to learn what each has to teach us. However, there is a common thread that underlies eating disorders and addiction: both gluttony and self-loathing are born of desire and lose their way not through their linkage with desire but with desire gone astray.

Desire for God

Christian theology has affirmed that human beings have a natural desire for God; they long to see God and to be in communion with God. The spontaneous desire for God is part of our human nature but cannot be fulfilled apart from God's own action. As a gift of God's redeeming grace, desire directs us toward God. By contrast, concupiscence, a concept Karl Rahner finds "surely one of the hardest in dogmatics," is identified as that which remains unredeemed and which must be struggled against.[27] It consists of those tendencies that direct us away from God.[28] Concupiscence directs the self toward making the self the object of fulfillment. We seek to consume enough, to earn enough, to be famous enough, to eat enough to be fulfilled. What is ultimately so tragic about concupiscence is that it destroys us rather than fulfills us. What we need is the redirection or transformation of concupiscence through and beyond ourselves and into a desire for God.

How can we assess the human desire for food in relation to sin and concupiscence? Is food by its very sensuality an object only of human concupiscence? We have said no and have affirmed, instead, the sensuousness and delight of food; we have affirmed the hunger for delight and sharing that God intends through food and eating. These are matters that have been redeemed by God and rightly direct us toward God. At the same time, however, food and eating can be misdirected; they can incline us away from God, away from delight and sharing, and cause pain and self-destruction and starvation.

Eating disorders may be sins against the self that are the result of under-esteem or contempt as much as they are of overestimation or hubris. While this may be true of individual sins, the injustices of the food supply system tend to be sins of greed or injustice, of overriding concern for self or devotion to one's own self-aggrandizement. To those global disorders we now turn.

5

Global Food Disorder

You're seeing people boycotting certain brands because they use slave labor or sweatshops, and we need to be thinking about this kind of thing much more with food. I mean, who is picking your food? What are the conditions under which they're picking your food? I absolutely think part of being alive and eating is thinking about how your food connects you to the rest of the world. And one of the exciting things about the community that feeds us, is that we are a community, and it behooves us absolutely to think about where that food came from.

—**Ruth Reichl, Editor, *Gourmet***

The economic benefits of world trade are a myth. The big winners are agribusiness monopolies that ship, trade, and process food. Agricultural policies, including the new Farm Bill, tend to favor factory farms, giant supermarkets, and long-distance trade; and cheap, subsidized fossil fuels encourage long-distance shipping. The big losers are the world's poor.

—**Brian Halweil**

WE HAVE BEEN using the doctrine of sin to help us understand the nature of individual eating disorders and have located two distinct kinds of eating disorder: gluttony or greed, and under-esteem or self-loathing. At base both are born of misdirected desire—in the case of gluttony, a drive to consume enough in order to feel good and to enjoy life; in the case of self-loathing, a desperate attempt to be enough (thin enough, pretty enough, bulky enough) to merit the acceptance of others. People with either kind of disorder cannot appreciate the food they eat for what it is—a part of God's grace meant for their enjoyment and sharing.

It is important for us to see how these disorders are encased in a wider system that promotes quite different values than delight and sharing, which are the central Christian values associated with food. Eating disorders are not individual deficiencies that somehow spring to life because of our own character disorders or sinful natures, but are nurtured and brought along quite carefully by myriad forces, only one of which is our own individual propensity toward self-justification. This chapter details the global system and lifestyle promotion that support eating disorders. The ultimate aim of this book, of course, is to suggest how we can delight in the food we eat and share it with joy. That will be impossible unless we can understand the social system that reinforces the distortion of desire that in turn gives birth to individual eating disorders.

The individual level we concentrated on in the last chapter is not disconnected from the global system. The two work in tandem. Without the global system promoting distortion, we could transform our individual desires more easily. Without the individual propensity to use food to try to satisfy desires, the global food system would not be fueled so continuously.

The Interconnection of Sinfulness

Recalling Aquinas's classification of sin as individual sin against the self (gluttony, greed), sin against others (murder, thievery), or sin against God, it becomes apparent in our present analysis that all three levels are all involved in the global food system. Individual disorders are related to systemic ones; sins against the self are also sins against others. Our analysis here will show how the system promotes disorder and sin against others. It is readily apparent that gluttony or overconsumption is one cause of the disorder of world hunger. But as our analysis progresses, I will argue that the disorders born of under-esteem and self-loathing are also related to the disordered state of the food system. The eating disorders of bulimia, anorexia, and obesity are exacerbated by our affluent society, to be sure. However, they evidence a complicity in the contemporary food system that destroys people and relationships, domestic and international. Clearly this violates both the norms of enjoyment and sharing.

We might conjoin two of Aquinas's categories and speak of social gluttony. Walter Rauschenbusch, in his book *Christianizing the Social Order*, spoke of the corporate nature of sin and how sin gets transmitted socially. It is just too simple to see overconsumption and under-esteem as only individual sins or character disorders. That is not helpful in any case. We are facing injustice on a global scale. It is a matter for worldwide analysis, because the system that puts food on the table of some is also depriving others of enough calories and nutrients to sustain life. This is a matter of justice and has been analyzed from a biblical justice perspective frequently and forcefully.[1] At the least, we can speak of injustice as depriving someone of the minimum necessities of life, when it is possible without undue hardship to provide such necessities or to help persons obtain them. As Rabbi Yachanon says, "To leave men [and women] without food is a fault that no circumstance attenuates; the distinction between the voluntary and the involuntary does not apply here."[2]

While the culpability for such injustice is diffuse, it is no less real. The system is a product of corporate decision-making; corporate bodies make and can transform their decisions. Those decisions, and eventually the system, are subject to human influence.

While it may appear that a discussion of the vast network of forces that make up the global food system is merely background and neutral analysis, with no bearing on our daily lives, we should recognize the sinfulness and self-serving that perspective of neutrality represents. Surely the analysis of the system does not exonerate us from our part in it. The system, after all, has its local outlet in the big-box stores or big supermarkets where you and I shop.

Hunger—The Extreme Disorder

If we begin at the most extreme evidence of disorder, then we must start with those 828 million people who are hungry, malnourished, and in danger of starvation. Every day more than 31,000 children die from hunger and other related, preventable causes. Nearly 160 million children are malnourished worldwide.[3] The most telling statistics I have read ask us to imagine that the globe is a small village of 100. If that were the case, there would be:

> 14 from the Western hemisphere, both north and south,
> 6 people would possess 59 percent of the entire world's wealth and all 6 would be from the United States,
> 80 would live in substandard housing,
> 70 would be unable to read,
> 50 would suffer from malnutrition,
> 1 would be near death; one would be near birth,
> 1 (yes, only 1) would have a college education,
> 1 would own a computer.[4]

Hunger or chronic undernourishment is related to any number of other social indications of life chances, such as the degree of wellness, sanitation, life expectancy, income level, and infant mortality. The evidence establishes a direct relationship between degree of nourishment and overall well-being. It is also true that there is sufficient food produced in the world to provide every man, woman, and child with 2,500 calories a day, a sufficient level for most adults.[5]

What underlies these statistics? There are so many factors that it is impossible to isolate any one; the truth is, I suspect, that even those most at the center of power are surprised by the extent of the influence that economic forces exert. Though there are personal and individual aspects of hunger, we will concentrate here on structural and global factors.

It is important to avoid demonizing any particular people or sector of society in our analysis. We must recognize that the forces that govern the global food market are such that, by the nature of their own rules, they are designed to grow and to accumulate capital, power, and market share. This is accomplished by charging a lower price for the same product or by becoming one of the few sources of revenue or supply.

Let me suggest first, in capsule form, some of the factors that produce hunger in the international arena and then factors closer to home. It should be clear that there is one interconnected global food marketplace and that its historical development is ongoing.

Globalization

The conglomerate of forces called "globalization" includes the so-called liberalization of world trade. The trade agreements that have been entered into and are under way at present are encouraged in the name of alleviating world poverty and hunger. All evidence, however, points to the contrary and suggests instead that globalization contributes to the increasingly wide gap between wealthy and poor countries.[6] The preferences provided to less developed countries (LDCs) in the form of lower tariff barriers are absent in sectors such as textiles or agriculture, where poor countries are best placed to expand exports. Take this example from the textile industry: "For every $1 provided to Bangladesh in aid, the United States takes away $7 through import barriers."[7] In the food industry, agricultural subsidies are most debilitating. Rich countries continue to subsidize their agricultural sectors munificently, flooding world markets with cheap grains. In effect, rich countries are discounting their exported foodstuffs. At the same time that the North is thus subsidizing its agricultural sectors, poor countries are forced to open up their markets to the world by the International Monetary Fund (IMF)/World Bank (the premier loan-making institution for LDCs). Because of subsidies in rich countries, small farmers in poor countries are undercut even before the markets open. They are forced to dramatically change their farming methods (usually not for the better), or else they are doomed to fail.

Globalization also increases hunger. When poorer nations are forced to "export crop" to pay off debts to the World Bank and other countries, production of food for subsistence has given way to crops that bring foreign exchange. The Pontifical Council for Justice and

Peace published a statement in January 1998 titled "Towards a Better Distribution of Land," which addresses this export cropping issue: "If the market prompts small farmers to grow export crops, this often takes place at the expense of production intended mainly for their own consumption, thus putting farming families at considerable risk. Unfavourable climatic or market conditions can lead to a vicious circle of hunger, so that such families contract debts that then force them to give up ownership of their land."[8]

Interrelated with hunger is, of course, the impact of farming practices on the environment. The latest specter now attracting attention is the supply of fresh water for irrigation that is decreasing around the world. This is becoming a major issue, especially in Asia where there is high demand for irrigation to grow rice and where the traditional sense is that farmers have a right to water.

The international food system links producers and consumers across geographical and political boundaries in such a way that those who can afford it can eat strawberries in winter and almost anything else at any time whatsoever. This involves immense amounts of fuel devoted to refrigeration, storage, transport, and communication technologies. We are eating higher on the hog, literally; more and more people are consuming meat. All this involves environmental stress, and the effort to produce what is merchandisable proceeds with no attention to pressures on soil or air or water unless there is a cost attached.

The global supermarket places major demands on the earth's ecosystem, demands that exceed what its renewable resources such as air, water, soils, forests, and fisheries can sustain. Twenty percent of the world's population lives a life organized around cars, meat-based diets, and disposable products (such as the packaging that adds appeal to our food). It is certain that all the people in the world cannot live at the level of people in the United States or the European Union. As a matter of fact, we who are the richest 15 percent consume 75 percent of the world's energy, much of that to grow and transport and fertilize crops. It would be impossible environmentally to sustain 6 billion or more people in this production and distribution system. Is it cynical to suppose that development policy has nothing to do with LDCs and everything to do with maintaining the lifestyle we citizens of affluent nations presently enjoy? Are we asking the poor of the world to produce food for us whether or not they can buy it themselves? At what social and environmental costs do we maintain our lifestyles?

"CHEAP" FOOD

The move toward globalization is accompanied by a search for the lowest-priced inputs. Like manufacturing and money, food industries are mobile and can spring up in any place where labor and raw materials and other costs are cheap. As a matter of fact, producing food at the lowest possible cost is considered a great good. Cheap food is a bargain, and we are addicted to bargains.

We in the United States boast that we spend only 11 percent of our income on food; in European countries that percentage rises to around 25 percent. The "cheap food" policies, endorsed by market capitalism and we who support that system, are not cheap for the environment, for farmers in LDCs, for communities who depend on food production, or ultimately for the health and safety of the food we eat. A cheap food policy puts pressure on food producers (who are increasingly large-scale operators who simply don't know the impact of fertilizers or biotechnology) to take whatever measures will enhance the bottom line rather than the value of the soil. Food is produced for export consumption, not for eating locally; if we knew where the food we eat came from and how it was grown, we might have second thoughts. If we had to eat what was grown locally, we might be more concerned about the health of the soil it grows in.

The mad cow disease, foot-and-mouth disease, and SARS epidemics we have encountered (and no telling what other global food epidemic since this writing) are evidence that the global supermarket is highly integrated and that it is difficult to escape a contagion that breaks out anywhere on the globe. This is yet another cost of cheap food for richer countries. When combined with poverty, this cost becomes even more serious. At the height of the mad cow epidemic, North Korea asked Germany to send the animals they were incinerating to them to assuage the hunger of the North Korean people.

CONSOLIDATION IN THE FOOD INDUSTRY

Finally, and related to all of the above, are the growing global business concentrations in the food supply industry. These concentrations, documented by William Heffernan and Mary Hendrickson for the United States,[9] are also evident in the grocery industry in the United Kingdom and in the increasing number of mergers and acquisitions throughout the world. (I am told that Wal-Mart is buying grocery stores in Scotland.) In 1995 the total value of mergers and acquisitions for the world exceeded any prior year by 25 percent.[10] Nearly every day the world press announces further consolidations, not least in food-related industries. The impact of this is that corporations have a great deal of influence globally. As a statement of the General Assembly of the Presbyterian Church USA put it: "Multinational corporations, whose influence in food production is global, are in the position to decide which people of the world will eat, as well as which farmers and ranchers—around the globe—will have access to the down stream market, thus exercising enormous control of food supplies."[11]

Domestic (U.S.) Disorder

We may be tempted to think that these are disorders that exist only on the international scene. However, despite the relatively strong economy that had until 2001 produced a boon for millions of citizens, there remained 31 million people in the United States who experience either food insecurity or actual hunger. *Food insecurity* is defined as lack of access to adequate supplies of nutritional food acquired without recourse to emergency resources like food pantries and soup kitchens.[12]

Many of those who experience food insecurity are the very people who grow our food. To be sure, poverty is the number one cause of hunger, but many family farmers—now called "growers"—are among the poverty statistics. How did this happen? It unfolded in many of the same ways that local producers worldwide became tenant farmers or landless. Now the specter is of farmers on food stamps.

In the past three decades agriculture has changed from a "family farm" organization that was hailed as the best, most efficient system on earth for the production of food and fiber. Not only did this system produce high-quality commodities, it also provided a good livelihood and life for many families and communities. It has—like many sectors of the economy—become industrialized. With the technological capability of producing food in large-scale operations came economic and ideological justifications for industrializing and then globalizing agriculture. The family farm structure of agriculture, the ethical values on which it is based, the content and nutritional quality of the food supply, and the lives of producer families and their communities were forever altered.[13]

The rapidly emerging structure of agriculture is industrial and global. It is controlled by a few multinational corporations who determine the world's food supply all the way from the patents for genetic material (seeds, pesticides and other chemicals, etc.) through the production, processing, and marketing of crops and livestock into the name brands in local supermarkets. These firms are interlocked with other companies and cooperatives. Everything is about "the bottom line"—the profit margin. Farmers are forced to buy inputs from and sell food production into the four to six food system clusters that no longer compete for the farmers' business. Most of the profits are siphoned off from the local community to shareholders. Only the price of labor stays at home while the farmers' expenses and debts keep growing. Every attempt is made to produce at the lowest price, which those of us at the checkout counter appreciate. In this system, however, everything is about producing cheaply. Nothing has intrinsic or God-given value. The cost of pursuing the only apparently lowest possible price can be quite steep.

In many ways this transformation is similar in its socioeconomic dynamics to what has been experienced in LDCs. The Presbyterian Church (USA) details some of the disordered consequences that result from this system domestically:

> The large scale corporate operation is often seen as a solution to our nation's goal of providing an inexpensive food supply to its citizens; however, large "farm factories" are creating new problems in rural communities in the areas of waste disposal, lack of anticipated community develop-

ment, and relocation of factories as they become obsolete or as lower paid workers in other regions of the world become available—all of which contributes to further dislocation of people and deterioration of community life.[14]

Those who promote large-scale hog operations, for example, work to put small operators out of business and depopulate the countryside so they can operate freely, without complaining neighbors. Such operations have a destructive potential for contaminating ground water and streams. Churches and many other institutions pay the price of social dislocations; our small farming communities are becoming ghost towns.[15]

Consolidation of corporate power has increased food insecurity, both the insecurity evidenced by hungry people but also the very safety of the food we eat. We remember numerous recalls of meat, the threat of bioterrorism, and quarterly reports of other threats. So many chemicals are used in food production now (for example, antibiotics in cattle and chickens) that most conventional food does much to poison us. It is clear that the safety of our food cannot be guaranteed. For example, Clifford Oliver, director of the U.S. Agriculture Department's office of crisis planning, warned, "We were coming to the realization that state and local government would be overwhelmed and the USDA would be overwhelmed if foot-and-mouth [disease] broke out."[16] Food security is threatened by the organization of the international food system. People throughout the world are increasingly dependent on a steady supply of food coming from long distances. "Driven by an economic model that emphasizes growth, comparative advantage and export production," writes Eva Jensen of Agricultural Missions, "governments increasingly fail to invest in community-based agricultural production and rural development to feed their populations."[17]

The cheap food policies and export subsidizing policies we have instituted appear not to have had the effect of driving out international competition as much as driving down the prices paid to small farmers around the globe. The large subsidies that the United States pays are going to the 2 percent of farms that provide over 50 percent of commodity and food sales.[18] At the same time, large farming operations and food corporations are reporting record profits. Is something wrong with this picture?

Impacts of the Corporate Food System

According to social critic William Greider, the "very sophisticated corporate system for food production is . . . creating new pockets of poverty across prosperous America—places where people without much income or influence dwell in an environment that is ruined both physically and socially."[19] Greider demonstrates that agribusiness is producing "messes" that parallel in a variety of ways those that government was making in "the coal and steel and other emerging [textile] manufacturing industries a century ago."[20] The policies that make for cheap food "assign its true costs to many unwitting victims," among whom are workers in the meat packing business, farmers, disadvantaged people who cannot successfully deflect toxic dumping in their communities, factory workers, the public health of all of us—from salmonella, antibiotic and hormone-fed meat, biotechnically produced foods (bovine growth hormones, genetically modified foods like StarLink corn)—and food security itself.[21]

FOOD INSECURITY

In regard to the latter, William Heffernan, a sociologist at the University of Missouri, suggests that "the control of the animal genetics pool is concentrating, and the genetic base for domestic animals is narrowing. For example, more than 90 percent of all commercially produced turkeys in the world come from three breeding flocks. The system is ripe for the evolution of a new strain of avian flu for which these birds have no resistance. Similar concerns exist in hogs, chickens, and dairy-cattle genetics."[22]

It is instructive that since the time of this writing, Hong Kong authorities slaughtered all poultry in that province to prevent the spread of avian flu,[23] and there was widespread slaughter of cattle in Great Britain to contain foot-and-mouth disease. The United States reported its first incidence of mad cow disease.

Food security is also threatened by the fragile economic condition of producers and great price swings. If there were two years of drought in a row, then farmers under contract ("growers") would slaughter their animals rather than feed them at a cost greater than they were being paid for finished animals . . . and there would also be food shortages! Finally, it must be said that part of the costs of cheap, corporate food policies is borne by the animals themselves who are often raised and slaughtered in ways that are cruel and inhumane. There are terrible stories of chickens stacked seven crates deep and of animals not yet dead traveling along slaughterhouse conveyor belts.

Public Health Issues

Then there is the quality of the food itself. We have a wider range of options for eating than ever before, and it appears that we are exercising those options more.[24] Americans spend half of every food dollar outside the home, eating Ethiopian, Indian, Middle Eastern, Afghan, Vietnamese, Mongolian, and Thai as well as Italian, French, and Chinese cuisine—and, of course, the omnipresent low-quality fast food. People in affluent nations are able to eat not only higher on the food chain but also more variety. Processed and prepackaged food choices have exploded. There are many restaurants vying to serve us breakfast, lunch, and dinner.

At the same time—remember, this is a chapter on food disorders!—there is an accompanying concern about the quality of the food we eat. "Because of changing food habits and more choices of foods, Americans may be more likely to get sick from what they eat today than they were half a century ago," reports the *New York Times*.[25] The frequency of serious gastrointestinal illness, one gauge of food poisoning, is 34 percent higher than it was in 1948, according to the Centers for Disease Control and Prevention.[26] In any given month, for example, nearly one-third of Americans have an episode of diarrhea.[27] Furthermore, as many Americans now die every year from obesity-related illnesses—heart disease and complications of diabetes—as from smoking.[28]

Eric Schlosser, author of the bestselling *Fast Food Nation*, has identified one culprit of this decline in public health: the high-fat, convenience food diet. He asserts: "Eating in the United States should not be a form of high-risk behavior."[29] Yet, it is. Obesity has been linked to heart disease, colon cancer, stomach cancer, breast cancer, diabetes, arthritis, high blood pressure, infertility, and strokes.[30] Schlosser's book also details some of the unsafe and unsanitary practices in the slaughterhouses and meat-packing plants of our nation that will make you sick.[31]

ENVIRONMENTAL IMPACTS

A final indicator of the systemic disorder is the price that the global environment pays for our food. For the sake of brevity, we will look only at how transportation and agricultural practices damage the environment.

Most food we eat travels long distances before reaching us. Each truckload of food produced in the United States travels from 1,500 to 2,500 miles to reach the supermarket. That is 25 percent farther than it was two decades ago. This reliance on long-distance food damages rural economies, provides numerous opportunities along the way for contamination, and contributes significantly to greenhouse gases (which in turn can affect our climate and ability to produce food). A head of lettuce grown in the Salinas Valley of California and shipped 3,000 miles to Washington, D.C., requires about thirty-six times as much fossil fuel energy in transport as it provides in food energy.[32] Or consider the typical can of diet soda, which contains one calorie of food energy: manufacturing "the can costs 800 kilocalories in fuel; involves land-destroying strip-mining; pollutes the soil, water, and groundwater with toxic materials; and uses up more water than the soda in the can."[33] These examples scratch the surface of the ramifications of what foods we choose to buy, where we choose to buy, the packaging of our food, and how we ourselves get to and from the store or market. (I had quite a different perspective after a year of carrying groceries by hand from the store a mile away from home!)

Shopping locally, eating less grain-intensive meats, walking or cycling whenever possible instead of driving, recycling, reusing containers for bulk foods, and buying directly from farmers—these can be enjoyable and healthy alternatives. They are ways that produce little pollution and involve the least possible expenditure of fossil fuels. Most of them also contribute to our fitness, involve meeting other people, and thus are friendly to us as well as to our earth. Energy conservation does not mean freezing in the dark or starving.

Agricultural practices—how our food is grown—contribute to negative environmental impact. There is evidence that the degradation to our earth community associated with agriculture—soil erosion, salinization, groundwater contamination, and climate change—is threatening the world's ability to feed its people. This linkage between hunger, poverty, and pollution underscores the need for sustainable agricultural practices. Farming that is heavily dependent on synthetic fertilizers, pesticides, and petroleum-based cultivation is also capital intensive and contributes to the loss of fertile farmlands and biodiversity. The industrial model of food production paves the way for disease; it entails feeding animals ten times the antibiotics humans use, and actually promotes illness.[34]

Industrial (or "conventional") agriculture destroys its own foundations. This method of food production accounts for about 20 percent of all fossil fuel consumption in the United States. Furthermore, the high costs of farming in this way and policies that reward large corporate farming drive out smaller farming operations. Although the number of farms has grown in the United States in the past decade, most of those are hobby farms that produce little food. There are far fewer farms where the owner-operators depend on the farm for their livelihood and contribute to the livelihood of the community.

It should be said bluntly: The way our food is produced, harvested, processed, and sold to us entails unsustainable cost to the earth community. This feeds into domestic (and worldwide) hunger and also into the diseased and malnourishing ways we eat.

Facing Complicity

Enough, you say. And I agree. I don't want to hear it either. There is a mountain of disorder; indeed, one might say that "the whole created order has been groaning in travail" (Rom. 8:22). We who are Christians also have the assurance that God will, in "the fullness of time," "gather up" and redeem all things (Eph.1:7-10).

Yet we are still forced to deal with *complicity*. This is a matter that all of us who are prosperous, who enjoy an overabundance of the good things of creation, need to confront for our own health and psychological and spiritual well-being. White males of a certain age have had to confront complicity in racism, sexism, and being citizens of a country at war with Vietnam, Iraq, and others. We continue to experience it in regard to world hunger. It is not direct guilt, it is not shame—it is complicity. This is a matter on which I have found little literature, but which is vital to understanding the disorder described in this chapter. (I hope others will build on this treatment of complicity, since it is widespread and deserves careful Christian attention.)

Let me illustrate. At a recent assembly of the European Christian Environmental Network in Raubichi, Belarus, near Chernobyl, the group visited the Museum of the Patriotic War in Minsk. The museum showed the atrocities committed by Nazi Germany against the citizens of Belarus in advancing through that country toward Moscow in 1941–1944. Photographs documented the hanging of young boys and girls, the massive execution of the large Jewish population of Minsk, death camps, and also the partisan resistance of the Belarussians against the Germans. The photographs were so graphic that I felt ill; the portrayal of resistance evoked admiration.

There was a large contingent of German pastors in the group, most of whom would have been children or younger during those years. On the way out, I talked to Pastor Stefan about how the museum affected him. What could one do about a sense of complicity in those atrocities? One response was to confess them, to remember them, and to ask God's forgiveness. There were also actions. It was clear that the German church had contributed much to the "Save the Children of Chernobyl Initiative" in Belarus and other rehabilitative efforts. I understood better why the German people had done so much in Belarus. There was a sense in which Stefan's and my conversation remained unfinished. Perhaps that was inevitable.

It is difficult to ascribe guilt to someone who did not directly cause harm, pain, or suffering. However, as members of a social group that has benefited to the detriment—harm, pain, or suffering—of another group, we feel some complicity in enjoying that benefit. For example, having been born into a United States middle-class Christian family has produced countless advantages for me. Should I feel guilty about those benefits? I think not. Should I recognize my complicity in systems that operate for my overabundance? Should I try to rectify some of those inequities to relieve hunger and other unjust distributions? As a Christian, it is my privilege to do so.

Just to expand the concept a bit, we notice that complicity *can* produce guilt when we neglect inequities or injuries—as did the priest who passed by the beaten man in the Samaritan parable (Luke 10:31). Complicity can also result in an immobilizing reaction; the problem can seem too overwhelming, too vast, too complicated for one person to do anything significant. I want to suggest that such avoidance or denial can have pernicious consequences for the complicit individual. It has worse consequences for the injured party, of course. But the denial of one's implication in an unjust system is a reaction that is self-reinforcing and often strengthens the injustice of the system. It also can become a nemesis for the perpetrator. Not taking account of complicity hurts our moral character. Easily imaginable is the erosion of our compassion toward the poor and hungry through a complicit habit of turning a blind eye to the beggar on the street. Less direct but possibly more destructive is our mindless enjoyment of the food we eat. Perhaps that mindlessness is due to a circumvention of complicity in a disordered system. It is possible, of course, that our enjoyment might increase into delight if we could rejoice in the justice of the system that produced a particular food.

Craig Nessan, a theologian, drawing on a comparison of the church's contemporary neglect of poverty and class divisions to the complicity of the "confessing church" in Nazi Germany, makes a direct application to the disorder of hunger. He asks, "As leaders in the church, how can we theologically and morally tolerate a status quo in which the reality of one billion malnourished human beings is considered 'normal'?"[35] Complicity is a corporate issue and not simply an individual one. The larger point is that we stand under judgment for passing by on the other side, for denying rather than facing and indeed embracing pain and suffering. (See Luke 11:37-52 for Jesus' list of judgmental woes to the Pharisees, and also verses 53 and

54, which record that from that time forward the Pharisees were "lying in wait for him, to catch him in something he might say." Such is the power of complicity.)

There are two faces to the complicity we practice in the global food disorder. These correspond to the two faces of individual disorder: greed and gluttony, and self-loathing and under-esteem. Complicity provides fertile soil for growing both the sins of gluttony and sloth. They also correlate—and this is a clue to the nature of complicity—to the twin purposes for which God created food: sharing, which corrects the sin of gluttony; and delight, which corrects the sin of self-loathing. Sharing and delight are the positive joys that gluttony and sloth destroy.

Addiction is aided and abetted by complicity. Indeed, our addiction to a comfortable lifestyle and neglect of global disorder may begin in the denial that is integral to complicity. (Perhaps that is why we are also so sensitive to criticism and so enamored of tolerating others. Otherwise, they might criticize us as well. We are anxious to obscure complicity.) We must develop habits of insensitivity and blindness if we hope to support our addiction. For example, and this one is too close to home, how many times have I had my cup of morning coffee and refused to acknowledge to myself how it was grown? Gluttony and addiction turn their backs on sharing or being aware of the environmental and human costs of our habits.[36]

Sloth, the traditional name for underachieving and underestimating one's God-given power, is first cousin to immobilization. (It is also another of the "deadly" sins.) Of course, immobilization in the face of massive systemic complexity may be due to the ways the system benefits us—at least in part. Sloth is the deadly sin that seduces us from compassionate action by cheapening God's grace and underemphasizing our empowerment by God. As Nessan puts it, "Our sloth steals from us any sense of urgency in responding to the needs of our hungry neighbors, replacing it with a sense of futility. We become indifferent, apathetic, spiritually dead."[37] That sounds very much like the opposite of delight to me. Such apathy may be born of the need to deny the contradictions of our lives. It begins to explain why our delight, our celebrating, our enjoyment may be minimal.

Nessan continues:

> In the case of starving people, the sloth of the comfortable
> is literally a deadly sin for those who daily perish . . . How
> severe will be [our] judgment if we neglect to feed our
> hungry neighbor! The response to the needs of the poor
> has consequences both for their salvation and ours: their
> physical condition is inextricably linked to our spiritual
> wholeness.[38]

The last two chapters of this book cover the ways in which men
and women deal with complicity and become partners with God in
furthering salvific work. Briefly put, this involves three steps: coming
to awareness, confessing, and repenting and being transformed.

The possibility of overcoming our complicity and lessening world
hunger may sound idealistic if not naïve. And so it would be had not
God redeemed the whole created order and were God not continuously beckoning all of us toward salvation. There is an Orthodox
metaphor that expresses the relation between human participation
and divine initiative. An iron that has been heated in the fire until it
is white hot can be molded and shaped. But when it is withdrawn
from the fire, it cools and hardens and cannot be shaped anymore.
Thus it is with our human participation in the fire of God: we are the
iron that can be transformed and used in many ways so long as we are
in the fire of God's presence and desire and purpose and will. Apart
from the directing and shaping of God's fire, we fall into mindless
grasping or obsessive addiction. Participating in God's directions, we
delight in eating and sharing food.

PART THREE

EATING FOR LIFE

Redeeming Our Lives

We can make the power of those who exploit us irrelevant.
. . . Choose to know the truth about global struggles, and
live in a way that supports a just alternative.

—Vandana Shiva
2002 World Social Forum

What if the self does not end at the borders of the body, but
is a small constellation of elements that includes those who
need us? If that were true, then, in taking care of others,
we'd be taking care of ourselves, too. Such care is rewarding,
nourishing. Women have always known this. . . .

—Alane Salierno Mason

Good Eating

I had been getting dismayed. Rome had been such a depository of
great places to eat and of neighborhood fruit, vegetable, and meat
shops. (Though we really didn't shop for meat very much, that was
not a terribly conscious or—horrors—"principled" decision.)

We had returned to the United States and the food seemed hur-
riedly and not very thoughtfully prepared. As a matter of fact, I am
tempted to call it "careless eating" as opposed to the "careful eating"

we experienced in Italy. I didn't want to turn into one of those "it's-always-better-overseas" Americans. Fortunately, then, I went to Shalom Hill Farm in Windom, Minnesota.

A group of theological educators who are responsible for teaching rural ministry had gathered through a Wabash College Center for Teaching and Learning initiative, and the site selected was Shalom Hill Farm. Mark and Margaret Yackel-Juleen are the directors of this retreat center/continuing education site. The buildings are built into the ground, and maximum use is made of solar, biomass, and conservation energy. Furthermore, though the retreat center requests that guests bag their linens and deposit them on the third-level laundry room, something about the way the request was made enabled me not to get reactionary about it. As a matter of fact, the tenor of the place—free from the distractions of television and the possibility of shopping—contributed to an appreciation of the panoramic vistas and also to a sense of being a participant in keeping the "farm" rather than being a consumer. It was peaceful, a retreat.

Now on to the food. This was careful food. Melinda, who did most of the cooking, also sold beef from her family's farm to Shalom Hill. Margaret and Mark raise a lot of the vegetables that go on the table. They also collect the eggs that go into the "egg bakes" that we had for breakfast twice. The food was not terribly sophisticated, but they did great things with it; for example, the pork roast was sumptuous—local pig helped, but Melinda said that she had a secret ingredient: red wine. Of course that's not the height of culinary refinement, but eating there made it clear that careful thought and care in preparation went far toward good eating.

Shalom Hills posted their food policy, which I think is worth sharing:

> Because we feel it's important to support agriculture which sustains the environment and those that live in it, we at Shalom Hill Farm are committed to using as many locally grown foods as possible. Many of our fruits and vegetables are grown organically either here at Shalom Hill, or on a nearby farm. All the eggs we consume are laid just yards from our kitchen by hens allowed to run around outside and scratch in the grass.

Our meats come from local farms where the animals live happy lives in the open air, free from hormone implants and force feeding. The coffee we drink comes from a fair trade coffee company which buys the coffee beans directly from farms in Third World countries, giving them a fair price for their beans, allowing them to use environmentally sound agricultural practices, and to live better lives.

By using these locally grown foods, we know we are offering our guests tasty, healthy meals as well as using food which is healthy and sustainable for our environment.

The Shalom Hill food policy made me feel good and eat well, which is hard to beat.

Trapped in Our Humanity

Unfortunately, the experience at Shalom Hill is all too rare for most people in the United States, let alone the world. This chapter will begin with two more common experiences: our entrapment in complicity even when we want to move beyond it and choosing to do what is not good for us. These common experiences lead to the recognition that we cannot change ourselves and that we stand radically and constantly in need of forgiveness. From the vantage point of God's forgiveness (justification), we can begin to move toward God in a fuller participation in God's design (sanctification). God became incarnate in Jesus the Christ in order to effect our redemption, so that we might respond to God's love in ways that reflect God's presence and purposes.

Caught between Systems

How are we to say grace over food disorders? How are we to recognize the presence of God's grace in a system in which close to a billion people are hungry or malnourished?

Christians are caught in the middle. They recognize that they are to live in this world as though in heaven, but they remain subject to all the desires and allurements as do others. They are caught in systems that are pleasurable and unjust at the same time. We will look here at two ways Christians are caught and how they try to free themselves.

COMPLICITY

The first continues our look at the problem of complicity in global and national systems. Judy Heffernan, director of the Heartland Network for Town and Rural Ministries, nicely encapsulates this problem of how to say grace in a complicit system. (Notice that the beginnings of redemption are present in the recognition of injustice.) She details aspects of the system over which we say grace:

- The centralizing of the global food system into the hands of a very few has forced and will force many "unneeded farmers" out of business. "When food is produced in this way and set before us, how shall we ask God's blessing on it?"[1]

- Farmers around the globe are being squeezed by cheap food policies, and immigrant laborers in fields and factories experience intolerable conditions. Poor people and rural communities wither and die as their means of economic support are destroyed. "How do we pray in the face of the social justice issues here?"[2]

- Environmental practices—such as building huge lagoons for animal waste that risk downstream life, increasing dependence for our livestock and plants on a tiny genetic pool, and tilling fragile soils—threaten many forms of life, including our own. "How do we pray as we confront the issue of environmental sustainability?"[3]

- Decisions about the food supply are made with very little democratic participation on the part of the landless, the holders of heritage seeds and breeds, and the continuously poor and hungry. "How do we pray as we confront these issues of human dignity?"[4]

- We whose pension funds are invested in and benefiting from the profits made in this system participate in it. We find it inconvenient to buy from farmers' markets. We go along with the ideology that this new system is inevitable, and that power is centralized. "How can we pray in the face of our own connectedness with sin?"[5]

Indeed, how can we ask God's blessing on this eating?

PERVERSITY

There is a second sin: loving that which is not good for us. Too often we reject those things that "are good for us." We are disordered as individuals; too often we practice perversity, or turning away from the good. Malcolm Gladwell captures this in a story he calls "The Trouble with Fries." He explains that a group of Auburn University scientists searched for a cooking oil that would give the flavor of fat without the unhealthy polysaturates in it. They were able to develop such an oil, and focus groups could not distinguish the healthy from the unhealthy, so alike were they. Then the McDonald's chain adopted this formula and began a product line that employed the healthier oil in cooking. This was, of course, the now-famous McLean DeLuxe version of their standard offerings.

People, however, stayed away from the McLean in droves. Gladwell hypothesizes that the name was a superfire way to kill the product: "sometimes nothing is so deadly for our taste buds as the knowledge that what we are eating is good for us."[6] Why do we reject what's "good for us"? There are several explanations. One focuses on our reaction against authority. When did Mom or another authority ever demand, "Now eat up all that candy and ice cream; it's good for you"? Another cause for rejecting what is good for us is the suspicion that the unhealthy tastes better. Conversely, when we know a product is healthier, we think it must not taste as good. Another reason we reject healthier food and are drawn to unhealthy food is simply because we don't listen to our bodies very well.

A final explanation for this perversity is worth noting in some greater detail because it intersects all of these. I believe the reason we like what is not good for us is that we have become persuaded that ours is a world of scarcity, and thus we think we have to grab the goodies before they are gone. A study by Leann Birch at Penn State examined children's expectations and eating patterns. Birch fed a large group of children a big lunch and then gave them access to a lot of junk food. She reported that "one of the things that predicts how much they will eat is the extent to which parents have limited their access to high-fat, high-sugar food in the past: the more the kids have been restricted, the more they eat."[7] To be sure, the kids were responding not to their own hunger but to the presence of food; they also assumed that anything restricted had to be good. Underlying all of these explanations, however, is scarcity. Advertising and other commercial appeals to this value are so pervasive that we fail to recognize them for what they are.

Beneath all of these explanations, however accurately they describe aspects of our behavior, our rejection of "what's good for us" remains somewhat mysterious. We simply have to acknowledge that we do what we know is not good for us, and we avoid the good that we know. And it's a time-honored problem; even the apostle Paul struggled with it! (See Rom. 7:15-20.)

Some experts have related this eating phenomenon to dieting, which they think *contributes* to obesity. They believe dieting teaches people to ignore their physical feelings and also disrupts their ability to handle normal emotions. People lose the ability to naturally regulate themselves.[8] Perhaps the Christian understanding of sin makes the Christian more realistic about the possibility of self-regulation!

The Way Out: Awareness, Confession, and Transformation

Both of these elements of sinfulness—getting trapped in complicity and perversity—bother me a great deal. I know about them quite well. The most difficult part is the complicated and entangled way that they involve me and how strenuously I have sought a way out. At some point I realized that I could not find my way out, not by myself and often not even in community. The only way out, I have discovered, is through God's forgiveness. It is impossible for me or for you to redeem myself/yourself.

AWARENESS

The first step out of these traps is awareness. This necessarily includes the notion of acknowledgment. We must be aware of our own involvement in the disorder of the food supply system and recognize that we cannot by ourselves become disentangled from it. We cannot effect our own justification or right direction toward God without God's initiative. We would find it difficult to even acknowledge our complicity in disorder or our perversity in rejecting the good were it not for God's action in Christ. Only God can save us from a crushing sense of sinfulness, whether of gluttony or self-loathing. Only God can save us to delight and share with joy.

God acts beyond our awareness, our acknowledgment, and our belief. God has already effected the redemption of the world in Jesus Christ. This does not depend on our awareness of it. (Whether we have to become cognizant of our salvation in Jesus Christ in order to be saved I confess not to know. To maintain that cognizance/confession is essential for salvation seems to me to assume knowledge that is beyond the human and approaches the divine.) In a way, it could be said that awareness is a passive activity; it is more a matter of consciousness than of overt action. Acknowledgment begins to be more overt, but both are less active than confession or repentance.

Awareness means being cognizant of God's initiative and acknowledging one's own limitations in the web of life. One becomes convinced of his or her own complicity and perversity in eating disorders. One also becomes convicted that it is impossible to extricate oneself from this sinfulness. Thus, the only way out is to be extricated from beyond oneself. One has to be aware that God has already redeemed us; God stands ready to forgive if God has not in fact already forgiven us. Sometimes God works through others to extricate us.

God's Accommodation

God has already blessed us and redeemed us. In numerous ways, we come to an awareness of these gifts of grace and an acknowledgment of our own disorder. Here we focus on three: God's accommodation to our human capacities; the gifts of animals, plants, and food; and the processes by which food becomes ourselves.

Our awareness begins with God's willingness to reveal the purposes of creation and our place in creation. John Calvin embraced and developed the concept that God accommodated himself to fit our human abilities.[9] God chooses to reveal herself to our limited understanding through the written word, through the book of nature, and also through other sources of wisdom. One of those is the *divinitatis sensum* or "awareness of divinity," which, according to Calvin, God implanted in each human being.[10] It may be that this awareness of divinity in God's grace-filled revelation was the first step toward redemption. Within this framework we can understand that an awareness and acknowledgment of food disorder is one way that God reveals herself to us. Food is one way God reveals gracious goodness to us. Thus God's blessing and redemption began with God enabling us to understand something of his own goodness and presence.

Recognizing Blessings

Earlier we claimed that one of the most pervasive theological themes in Scripture was that the world is a gift, a blessing to us. We can lose sight of this. It is an aspect of God's redemption that becomes assumed and thus taken for granted. It escapes the level of our awareness. An excellent example is that we lose sight of the very food that we eat. We lose sight of the fact that the food we eat was alive not so very long ago. It had a life that transcended our own and had intrinsic, and not simply utilitarian, value. Our socialization has turned chickens into "fryers," pigs into "pork," and radicchio into "salad." Having lost touch with the source of our food, we tend to lose touch with its giftedness as well. Social ethicist Howard Harrod observes:

> Especially in urban centers, many generations of children have matured into adulthood without any primary experience of domestic animals and no practical knowledge of where food products such as milk or eggs originate; they have seen neither milking nor egg laying. Even further from the experience of such persons is the reality of slaughtering animals for food. Nutrition and food con-

sumption are understood more in terms of vitamins, calorie intake, and fat content. The living animal as well as the
blood, entrails, and hair out of which meat products
emerge are matters far from the consciousness and practical experience of most people. . . .[11]

We have lost a sense of relationship with the plant and animal
kingdom whose members have much in common with us. Reducing
the source of our food to their brand names or corporate sponsors
makes us lose sight of the ways in which we are gifted by God rather
than by Del Monte, Tyson Farms, or IBP.

Awareness of the way that God has provided us the gifts of animals
and plants that are sacrificed for our well-being and are easily and
deliciously appropriated as food is part of our becoming whole persons. We need to appreciate that part of our redemption. I confess
that, even though my father raised chickens and we had a large garden while I was growing up, I frequently forget what it is that I am
eating and how this created goodness got to my body.

"Is not the rest of creation redeemed?" my theological ethicist
wife asks me. That is the biblical witness: with the incarnation of
Jesus Christ the whole created order has already been redeemed.
What that means is difficult to put into words. Creation can be
tainted; it can be subverted. The purposes for which God created
plants and animals can be perverted. The creation is not yet, any
more than us, fully redeemed. I do not think that trees or animals are
agents in the same way that humankind is, but I do think that all creation stands under the need to be redeemed, to be restored to the orig-
inal state of *shalom*. In some cases, the redemption of plants,
animals, rivers, the land, and other creatures is radically interconnected with human agency, fallenness, and redemption. We talk of
the regeneration of land, rivers, plants, animals, and the way in
which God redeems and stands ready to redeem us beyond our conscious intentions or participation. Especially striking to me are the
natural processes of creativity and regenerativity that are built into
the land, into animals both human and nonhuman, and into rivers
and plant life. Sometimes, many times, we do nothing; God does all
the redeeming. We do not even, cannot even, participate in it.

I believe that God works this way with us as well. Sometimes, perhaps always, we are redeemed beyond ourselves with no conscious effort on our parts. Certainly this is beyond conscious participation. How do our cuts and scratches get healed? Think of all the involuntary ways we are sustained and restored—regenerated, if you will.

Everyday Miracles

A third step of becoming aware includes the very miracle of the processes by which food becomes myself. Eating food is the miracle by which we take the world into ourselves, allow it to be transformed into our body-selves, and then go back into the world where we use it to make other food and also make love, make politics, and make changes. The complex bodily and earthy growth and sustenance processes are so integral to our natures that we easily lose our wonder at these marvels. Being brought to a re-awareness of this divine ecology that we embody in concert with the earth is itself a gift of awareness.

Notice that we are involuntary recipients of these three aspects of reality. We simply receive them. We cannot fail to receive them as capacities and parts of the world we inhabit. We are thrown into this goodness. It is, of course, possible not to come to recognition or appreciation, but some theologians like Calvin and Jonathan Edwards claimed that it is impossible to completely squelch our sense of the divine.[12]

The capacity to be aware of these and other kinds of divine gifts is itself undeserved. As we do become aware of them, however, that awareness of God's ongoing providence for all species and for us casts a harsh light on the way we have responded to God's care, especially how we have cared for the animals and plants whose sustenance is our responsibility and the care with which we live our lives. Part of coming to awareness is a positive appreciation of all God has given us. That very sense of wonder and gratitude also enables us to acknowledge that we have not lived in ways that respect the marvels of life. We acknowledge that we have sinned and fallen short of caring for God's creation. This first step—awareness/acknowledgment—

moves us beyond complicity and toward wholeness. How we come to this awareness and acknowledgment is itself a gift of grace; it is also a mystery.

CONFESSION AND REPENTANCE

The second step toward our appropriation of God's redemption follows on the heels of awareness. With acknowledgment of the graces we have already received, we acknowledge the power and love of God and our own failure to live in ways that are appropriate responses to the wondrous world and bodies that we enjoy. We sink our teeth into a Chilton County (Alabama) peach and, with the juice dripping down our chins, we break into "How Great Thou Art." We also come to recognize that we didn't do anything to produce these beauties and that such delight comes to us unbidden. How we live in the face of such goodness evokes an acknowledgment of our finitude and also of how far we are from living with the care that such a good world deserves.

The moment of confession is itself the threshold of forgiveness. Coming to awareness of God's many graces and, simultaneously, our own ingratitude and injury to self and others is painful because it moves us to acknowledge our personal blessings of food and life and also our personal complicity in sin. True awareness and acknowledgment is "up-close and personal," a heartfelt experience rather than a cognitive bit of information that we can hold at a distance.

Human beings who become aware of their complicity in unjust systems could not come to confession without the hope of forgiveness. Just as an awareness of grace is essential to an acknowledgment of guilt, so also is the assurance of pardon essential to confession. We would be crushed by our injustice or compelled to deny, avoid, displace, or otherwise discount our own complicity were it not for God's compassion. If we did not know that Jesus Christ came to save sinners, we could not repent and confess. We would have to hide from the truth.

It is God's great goodness and love that enable us to repent and confess. As painful as it is to become aware of and acknowledge our own hypocrisy and contribution to evil, just as great is the relief of knowing that Jesus Christ became incarnate to bring us to repentance and beyond. "In the cross of Christ we glory," as the hymn goes. The cross stands as the symbol of faith in part because there the compassion of God is fully tangible. We can feel it in our bones. Assured of the possibility of forgiveness, we can confess.

The goodness of food, an incarnation of God's grace, can remind us of the grace of Jesus Christ. Good food and delightful meals can remind us of the many ways God's grace becomes incarnate in our lives. Furthermore, sharing such food can be a gracious sharing, an act of compassion to others because of the compassion that we have received from God and God's people.

Bodily Confession

Sometimes the act of confession is an intense rush of emotions— clarity, guilt, gratitude, joy. It is bodily. We feel God's grace and we cry out our confession, almost rejoicing. Such moments sustain what could become routine confession in the act of worship. Many women theologians are reminding us how important it is to feel God's goodness bodily, to *know* God as well as to reflect *about* God. Lisa Dahill argues, "So it is vital to begin here, in our bodies and their struggles, if we are to experience the real love of God and meet other Christian women and girls at the center of their embodied, spiritual need."[13] Men and boys, of course, need to know God bodily as well.

Perhaps our bodies are the very place where God indwells our lives. It is difficult to imagine God indwelling in a way that did not somehow manifest bodily. The hungry ghosts that we want so much to avoid may acquire their power precisely through our avoidance of bodily attention. We fear becoming aware of those ghosts or acknowledging them, much less confessing them. But maybe they are the means by which God is calling us to confession, repentance, and redemption. They represent bodily cravings. They may be the openings to our infinite hunger for God. They may be leading us through the body's incarnate wisdom toward God's nurturing presence. It may be when we feel "beyond the pale" of salvation that our bodies are calling us beyond dependence on our own performance. The late French religious and social thinker Simone Weil recounts an instance when she was experiencing profound suffering: "Moreover, in this sudden possession of me by Christ, neither my senses nor my imagination had any part, I only felt in the midst of my suffering the presence of a love, like that which one can read in the smile of a beloved face."[14]

Sometimes the wisdom of the body calls us to God through the cravings of hungry ghosts or suffering, but sometimes, in contrast, the wisdom of the body calls us to God through beauty or enjoyment or sharing. We recognize grace, we say grace, and we are opened to God's breath from on high in many ways. Most of them—I am tempted to say all of them—involve our bodies in some way. Often we see our bodies as limiting and confining and restraining us—if no longer as a source of sinfulness. However, our bodies with their limits are important means by which we are brought to redemption. Tempting as it is to contrast confining limits with that which brings us to redemption, the truth may be that it is *through* our limits, our bodies, that we see our needs. It is also through our bodies, our limits, that we experience joy and meaning.

Three or four decades ago, many Christian theologians were timid about incarnation; they shied away from claiming or proclaiming the bodily presence of God. In doing so, they forgot the work of the Spirit. However, in the past two decades, the body has been resurrected as a place where God is significantly active. Ecological and feminist theologians have alerted us to the centrality of God's incarnate presence. The quite tangible way that food becomes enjoyed and embodied reminds us of God's grace, nurturing and sustaining us. This reminder promotes confession and it also reinforces our awareness of God's grace.

Many times, of course, we feel trapped in a system where our easy participation adds to the problems. We do not intend to perpetuate such injuries. We certainly do not mean to harm ourselves. Our confession may well encourage us to resist participating in this system. We still feel the lure of gluttony, tempting us to "live by bread alone." We are still tempted to substitute love of food and pleasure for the love of God. We still forget the hungry neighbor.

True confession born of repentance makes us uneasy with such continuing temptation. We recognize our limits but have now been freed to resist entrapment. We are encouraged and encourage each other to resist evil and complicity, as well as to delight and share. We learn to live in the tension of being justified, but still sinners.

TRANSFORMATION

Repentance leads to confession and to assurance of pardon. A third step is transformation: we change and we continually ask God to help us change. Genuine repentance and confession make us resolve to move Godward; over time we develop habits that begin to change our way of living. We change our practices. As farmer, writer, and social critic Wendell Berry says, a "change of heart or of values without a practice is only another pointless luxury of a passively consumptive way of life."[15] Berry is right: we have to practice what we confess if we want our confession to mean anything at all, to us and to others. We need to confess with our bodily practices.

Beyond the hypocrisy of repenting without changing those practices that led us to repent, there is an inherent desire to continue depending on ourselves. When we succumb to this, we are not really responding to God's goodness. We cannot really say grace. Most strongly put, we are still lost in our own desires. We blindly continue to pursue our own directions and try to create our own grace.

Finally, transformation is about our own healing. Repentance and confession put us on the right track. During those times when we feel tugged between self-dependency and God-dependency, Christian practices such as prayer and fasting are important ways of keeping us in touch with our spiritual selves. In traditional language, justification precedes sanctification.

This three-phase sequence of coming to claim our redemption presents a paradox. (At least it is a paradox in the context of the culture of the contemporary United States and other affluent nations.) We are a "cheap grace" culture. We believe that redemption and salvation are on one end of a continuum and at the other end of the continuum is suffering and pain and the negations of life. It is difficult to imagine redemption as involving the acknowledgment of evil and sin in ourselves, others, and the world; we believe that redemption should be totally pleasurable and happy. Redemption should also be under our control.

What I have found, quite in contrast, is *that the process of delightful redemption is accompanied by the acknowledgment of sin, the confession of that personal sin, and transformation in directions that involve effort and growth.* The process that has been described in this chapter has focused on complicity, precisely because the acknowledgment of that complicity is not fun. It is not pleasurable because it involves recognition of our own deficiencies and proneness to sin.

Dependency

While God's twin purposes of delight and sharing may seem at times to be easy and nonthreatening, I suspect otherwise. Truly saying grace and truly confessing and turning in holy directions involve dependency. Things are not under our control, which makes us uncomfortable. We are forced to recognize that we must live out our obligations, our indebtedness, and our giftedness. Food and the delight we can experience at mealtime come from beyond ourselves; to truly say grace we have to recognize all of food's origins, primarily in God.

There is a mystery about food and also about the paradoxical nature of redemption. It is almost as though there is a second level of enjoyment more profound than the first which can be identified only as a sensation. While there is much that is enjoyable about sensation, there is a much deeper sense of delight and more delightful sensations when we acknowledge our sin and turn to God to transform us. That transformation ushers in a greater sense of completeness, of wholeness, of integrity. Indeed, food can be a symbol of providence, of our own being totally cared for beyond our own control or knowing. Perhaps the paradox can be explained, though not resolved, by seeing delight and accountability, confession and transformation as conjoined and mutually dependent.

Praying and Fasting

There are many ways in which transformation can occur. Most of the examples I will give tend to be relatively individual, though the first example of saying grace is usually a social practice as well.[16]

Consider what happens in the simple act of praying before meals. When we say grace, often as not we say to God something like: "bless this food to our use, and us in thy service." This acknowledgment of our being blessed and forgiven "in Christ's name" is an act of worship. It moves beyond self-dependence toward an active appropriation of our forgiveness. Saying grace before meals may also include a petition for God to strengthen us for service and discipleship. Part of that service and discipleship has to do with sharing our talents, energy, and resources with others. Thus the act of saying grace acknowledges God's goodness and offers a response to that goodness in our transformation.

A second example of a transformational practice—fasting—makes the point that delight and confession go together. At first sight, fasting seems to be the opposite of delighting in good food. However, I think the real opposite is mindless eating or not knowing where food really comes from (notwithstanding the fact that we cannot know where food comes from, finally, except from God). Fasting is a spiritual discipline that sharpens the delight of eating. In chapter 1, we speculated about what food meant to those who had never been really hungry. Fasting is a discipline that enables us to approximate the state of being really hungry. "If you never fast," writes pastor Mark Buchanan, "then the whole concept of being wholly nourished and sustained by God's word will be only a nice, sweet and totally irrelevant thought. You may pay the idea lip service, but you'll be too busy licking sauce off your lips to do any more. And worse: if you never fast, you may not stand when the day of testing and temptation comes."[17]

Fasting is all about seeking God's guidance; it is a hungering and thirsting for the Spirit of God—a hunger for more of God's direction in our lives. Fasting, according to Buchanan, is a means whereby God orchestrates hunger to humble his people. Fasting shows us our limits and dependency. Discomfort evokes the realization of our frailty as well as the urgency of others' hunger, especially when that hunger is involuntary.

Second, fasting tests what is deep in our hearts. We deprive ourselves of confronting who we are when we feed every craving. We cannot allow delight to emerge because we smother it with immediate gratification. We don't trust that what might emerge in our fasting could enrich and really feed us. Fasting also reveals that we live not by bread alone, but by the bread of true delight, by the hunger for God. It is God who has the words of eternal life and of salvation here and now. The deepest need we have is to be in covenant with God, to feast with Jesus as Jesus feasted with all. We need to share and to live now as though in heaven, as though at the Messianic banquet.[18]

Pastor Garret Keizer suggests that we tend to live by the motto "If it feels good, do it." That is "just another way of saying, 'If it tastes good, eat it.' In America it sometimes seems that on these two commandments hang all the law and the profits."[19] Keizer suggests that it might be time to bring back some dietary laws, that a few carefully selected dietary restrictions prayerfully chosen—for instance, not eating chickens that were unjustly raised and processed, or eating close to the source of local supply—might turn the tide. The witness of "two or three refusals as simple and quiet as a child's table grace, and the world would stand amazed. Behold, the kingdom of God remains in that place where Jesus put it on the night in which he was betrayed—in fact, where most of the other things we lose sight of are bound to turn up—right on the kitchen table."[20]

Transformations in Attitudes

From these two practices—saying grace and fasting—we turn to some attitudes that represent transformations. The two attitudes, or dispositions that flow from the salvation offered by God in Christ, are contentment and generosity. These are not the virtues held in highest esteem in our culture, but they are profoundly valuable.

The first—contentment—is associated with a basic satisfaction with one's life. This is an attitude that is very much in short supply in our nation, so much so that it usually connotes a lackadaisical attitude or complacency. In truth, contentment is based on a peace with oneself and an acceptance of who one is. In regard to food and eating this is a hugely significant attitude. A basic issue underlying women's eating disorders is a serious discontent with who they are and with their lives. This discontent is just as much a male issue, except that its remediation tends to be poured into achievement-orientation as much as it is into obsessiveness about appearance and being buff. (The issue of bodily appearance and looking good and powerful is clearly important to junior high, older youth, and men in general.)

Contentment is anathema to the advertising industry; in fact, creating discontent is what sells cars and deodorant and perfume and diet regimes and low-fat products of every type. However, having created that discontent, most ads end with the consumer arriving at the desired state of contentment, whether that is associated with having bought the right product or becoming the new, slim me that is attractive to everyone of the preferred sex. The power of advertising is so pervasive that often it disguises from us what we really need and who we really are. That is, it makes us discontent with who we are and what we have. It misidentifies our discontent and what will fulfill our discontent—which is finally only communion with God.

The transformation wrought by redemption changes us from feeling that we have to be slimmer or more beautiful or have more friends to be acceptable and contented. In Christ, we are able to be more contented with who we are, to forgive ourselves as Christ forgives us. We confess, we are forgiven, and we attempt to change to live a more Christian life. In saying grace, we affirm our blessings and also our intentions to live the new life in Christ. We can live more at peace with God and ourselves (Rom. 5:1-5; 6:1-6). Our attitude changes from a basic discontent to a basic contentment. That attitude enables us to have a more realistic sense of what is worth changing and what we really need. It enables us to enjoy our lives more, including our bodies and our eating. It disarms the demon of discontent (or self-loathing) that engenders eating disorders. It may promote delight by rightly directing us to God and neighbor.

The second attitude of transformation is generosity, which encourages sharing and undercuts the sin of gluttony. With this attitude, our eating changes from eating graspingly to eating graciously and generously. Rather than hoarding from others or having to have the best for ourselves, we build on the attitude of contentment, which promotes respect for one's body and appreciation for what food is and where it comes from. Understanding who we are and that we have "enough" because of God's grace, we can share that goodness with others. Contentment with one's self transforms a preoccupation with self into a more generous attitude toward others.

Our redemption moves us to life according to the Spirit of Jesus, who was uniquely generous and compassionate toward others (Rom. 8:5-11). Many biblical scholars have commented on Jesus' generosity to all people; all are invited to eat with Jesus. Jesus seems always ready to share whatever is available with everyone. Most particularly at the Last Supper, Jesus is the gracious host sharing all that he was with others. We understand that the "new life in the Spirit" is about being as generous to the neighbor as we are with ourselves. Furthermore, Christian tradition underscores that the Spirit assists us in living more and more contentedly and generously.

Gardening and Cooking

Two specific activities "feed" transformation: gardening and cooking. These activities are not transformations inherent in redemption, but rather two examples of food activities that reinforce the transformational practices and attitudes just described. They are activities that can be commended for developing Christian virtues, such as patience and appreciation. In other words, they are more optional activities than they are practices or attitudes. Nevertheless, many people do garden to some extent, and almost all people prepare food; thus, they are fairly common, routine activities.

Many authors who write about food suggest that everyone ought to grow some of the food they eat. Indeed, gardening teaches us where food comes from and the sort of effort it takes to put food on the table. It reminds us of the important combination of soil, sun, and sweat and how rewarding the products of raspberry bushes, tomato plants, and cornstalks can be. In *Soul Gardening: Cultivating the Good Life*, Terry Hershey emphasizes another powerful aspect of gardening: how gardening cultivates us:

> To be human is about gardening the soul. You can count me in if it means cultivating a place where I am attentive, present, and grounded. It's just that twenty years of relentless pursuit of the good life delivered by a lottery-driven culture has rendered my perspective noticeably one-dimensional—what's the payoff?—as if consumption equals life at its finest. Now, my questions have begun to change: Are there butterflies in your garden? . . . Do sunsets make you smile? . . . Have you ever watched the hummingbirds dance?[21]

The point of gardening is for the sheer love of it, she says, and the discovery of who you are and where you are rooted when you give yourself over to gardening. "Gardening is about seeing. Gardening is about awareness. . . . It is the difference between managing life and entering into life. . . ."[22] I love the naked appreciation and sheer wonder Hershey feels in the presence of growing plants, the delight that he takes in gardening and the appreciation he shares with us. Indeed, I will probably give myself over to gardening a bit more. It is transformational.

Another transformational food-related activity is cooking. My family teases me that when my wife, Patti, started commuting to Chicago, I would grill eight hamburgers at a time. My son, Nate, and I would eat two, and I would save the other six for the next three nights. It was ugly. In my defense, however, I do know good cooking when I taste it. Italian cities are a collection of great restaurants and fruit and vegetable markets, all of which I love and know well. I tend to identify European cities by their restaurants and specialties. My grandmother used to cook so joyfully and enthusiastically that sometimes I wonder whether it was her singing in the kitchen while we "helped" or the food itself that was so delicious. It is merely academic to try to separate those two.

In the book *Chocolat*, author Joanne Harris describes the main character, Vianne Rocher's fascination with cooking:

> There is a kind of sorcery in all cooking; in the choosing of ingredients, the process of mixing, grating, melting, infusing, and flavoring, the recipes taken from ancient books, the traditional utensils. . . . And it is partly the transience of it that delights me; so much loving preparation, so much art and experience, put into a pleasure that can last only a moment, and which only a few will ever fully appreciate. . . . I stole menus from restaurants and looked longingly into patisserie windows. . . . I carried recipes in my head like maps. All kinds of recipes: torn from abandoned magazines in busy railway stations, wheedled from people in the road, strange marriages of my own confection. . . . Cookery cards anchored us, placed landmarks on the bleak borders. Paris smells of baking bread and croissants; Marseille of bouillabaisse and grilled garlic. Berlin was Eisbrei with sauerkraut and *Kartoffelsalat*, Rome was the ice cream. . . .[23]

If ever there was an activity capable of combining delight and sharing, it is cooking. Good food prepared with real love for those who are to eat it and also with an awareness of its source—surely that is close to heaven. What such preparation does to the formation of the cook and also to those who enjoy the results of such care is an ordinary miracle. The careful preparation of a meal can be a spiritual discipline by which the cook links the things of God with the things of earth. There is clearly a corporate dimension to these practices, attitudes, and activities, which will be discussed in the following chapter.

A New Vision
for the Church

The table, the trough, has God's fingerprints all over it. We participate in a mystery whenever we eat food. Indeed, every meal is sacramental. Through eating, death is resurrected into life. Dead fish, dead figs and dead cornflakes are transformed into the living tissue of our bodies. Through some mystery brewing deep inside of us, all that dead matter comes to life. . . . That is an event I would call sacred—a holy occurrence.

—Kelton Cobb

I'M SURE I've been spoiled. If there is a gastronomic world center, it probably isn't too far from Rome. But Rapallo, Aix-en-Provence, and Geneva also offered great restaurants. We lucked into two great places in Rapallo, Italy.

We arrived back in the United States, back to Dubuque, Iowa. Home. Have you ever landed at an airport with a bounce rather than a gentle put-down? Have you ever wobbled a bit on the runway before straightening out? Ours was a bit of a hard landing, culinarily speaking. Fortunately our friend Judith Porto Shepherd was there. She eased our re-entry with her marvelous salad—gentle rubs of whole garlic around the bowl first—and other creations. However, in the universe of eating, Dubuque is not in the first rank.

What struck me most forcefully was that people do not take the time to eat. They rush into a restaurant with only a certain amount of time before returning to work or another engagement. In Italy eating *is* the engagement. Also, in Italy there is nothing very serious scheduled after lunch or dinner—after a 1:00 p.m. *pranzo* there is at least a bit of a *riposo;* after *cena* at 8:00 or 9:00 p.m. there is conversation, recreation, walking, sleep. (Interestingly, Italians do seem to breakfast on the run.) Eating is not the event in the United States that it is in Italy. This is, I fear, a bit of an idealized account, but on balance eating doesn't seem to be given the same priority in the United States. While you may be thinking this is a trivial issue, for me it represents a real loss of time for socializing and also for sheer enjoyment.

Another eye-opener was my local, fairly routine U.S. supermarket. I had gotten used to the SMAs (supermarket equivalent) and to my neighborhood stores in Rome. The supermarket five minutes from my doorstep in Dubuque is huge and beautiful by comparison. It has ten feet of shelf space devoted to salad dressings, and probably twelve brands of peanut butter (each with crunchy, creamy, and low-fat variations). There are cheeses in multiple packages; lots of produce, milks, and breads—a veritable cornucopia.

And so much of the food is fat-filled. Even at the Mexican restaurants—which we missed while in Rome—the chips and fried chimichangas and taco salads are not health foods. The ubiquitous hamburgers and fries fairly leap with saturated fat. And yes, the diets at these restaurants show. People are heavy. I personally know fat, and it's not like I hate chimis, chips, or burgers. But Americans are fat. Especially noticeable were younger kids and the people I encountered shopping at discount stores late at night, which is to say working class and poor people.

So you figure it out. Eating is not accorded much status or time: meals are often eaten quickly, and there is a premium on speed. We found ourselves getting swept into this mode. The supermarkets are filled with a great choice of beautiful foods in multiple packages. Really, grocery shopping has long been one of my favorite things. Then, added to the mix, is the fat-filled diet we are on, and the way we eat too much of the things that make for obesity. Our family found ourselves moving back into this old eating program rather quickly. On the one hand, there is in the United States an appreciation for and abundance of food; on the other, little attention is given to what we eat or how we eat it. How does this inconsistency happen? What is the way out of this trap?

Perhaps it is because we live at such a frenetic pace that we fear not being able to try everything. We want to experience it all. We look at a menu or walk though a supermarket and we are tempted by everything; we want to consume it all—now! Very much connected to this, I fear, is the loss of the ability to enjoy. In a consumption mode, we expect those things that we pull into ourselves (those things we "ingest") to satisfy us. We expect that they will enable us to enjoy ourselves. It is almost as though by making them part of ourselves, we will in fact ingest enjoyment. This business of "ingestion" is basically a mechanical image, which suggests an entity without the capacity to enjoy. Is this the way we see ourselves? By contrast, enjoyable ingestion does require a recipient *with the capacity to enjoy* the good things of food, travel, and friendship. Enjoyment is in no way automatic: it cannot be bought or simply consumed. When exacerbated by a consumption mode of enjoyment, the pace of our lives creates time pollution. We seem not to live in the present long enough to be able to enjoy without thinking toward the future.

What most alarmed me upon returning was that my own resolutions about walking to the grocery instead of driving the car, and about eating in a relaxed and healthy way, went out the window. My own struggles with weight and firm resolves were getting sucked into a whirlpool of cultural forces. Eating at fast-food burger chains, Mexican restaurants, and nicer sit-down chains all conspired to move me away from my resolves. The *force*, the *power* of cultural group norms was alarming.

It probably should not have surprised me so much; after all, those norms were simply suspended a bit for the year we lived in Europe. Then they returned with a vengeance. The fact is that the economic and social structures—of supermarkets, of time allocation and priority, of restaurants, and diet, of marketing, of personal lifestyle habits—are mammoth. They are pervasive and reinforced by media, by habit, by social groups, and by institutions. (For an alternate set of

norms, consider the Shalom Hill Farm food philosophy in chapter 6.)
The culture of eating itself was so strong that it literally felt like I had
been dropped into a river and the current had picked me up and was
pushing me in its own directions.

I have seldom, if ever, had such a vivid sense of the power of group
norms that shape my life. If I am to change my habits, if I am to learn
to enjoy more, then it will take a group to stand against and modify
the cultural forces that have shaped my eating and affect my ability
to delight and share.

Community Power

Chapter 6 may have given the impression that salvation is an individual occurrence rather than a communal one. It might have sug-
gested that redemption is a once-for-all event rather than an ongoing
dynamic. The present chapter will suggest how thoroughly communal the process of salvation is and how we in the church might discern and promote God's activity. It will focus on how communities
in the culture, but especially the church, mediate God's grace and
God's redemption.

I suspect that most of us learned early that it was natural and
enjoyable to eat with others. We may have been taught that smoking,
drinking, cursing, having sex, or being too raucous was wrong, but I
suspect that most of us also learned that food was okay—a good
thing, and that it was unnatural not to enjoy eating. We learned that
from eating with others. Our grandmothers may have been gleeful
when they were about the business of feeding us. Mine certainly was!
But we also learned that we should eat everything on our plates. In
that way you appreciated the cook and also didn't waste the precious
commodity of food. We also learned that it was wrong to eat in front
of others without sharing; that it was stingy and not what Christians
or "nice" people did.

The point here is that the community—whether the church or
other social associations or the culture in general—has power to shape
the sorts of meanings and norms we internalize about eating. Furthermore, the communities to which we belong continue throughout

our lives to shape our attitudes and practices. Like it or not, the culture we live in shapes our thinking and our feeling. To be more precise, the communities we inhabit, inhabit us. We are the fish that have learned to swim but are not aware of the medium they swim in. A certain humility about how much we can control is in order.

Fat Land by Greg Critser does a truly remarkable job of showing how institutions—business corporations, the loss of physical education requirements, the rise of media inactivity, even the church—have contributed to obesity.[1] The book demonstrates persuasively that the culture as a whole has shaped us beyond the level of the individual. This strongly suggests that there must be a communal dimension to reversing the cultural pressure to overeat and underexercise. And this at a time when some are saying there has been a decline in our "social capital" or community. I suggest that the church is a community that can resist cultural pressures—indeed, it must resist many of those pressures. And the pressure to overeat may be one of those.

We live in a culture—as most affluent people do—that has touted the values of achievement and "getting ahead," which usually means becoming wealthy and achieving an upscale standard of living. What that "upscale standard of living" might include can be gauged from the advertising wars in which automotive, exercise equipment, cosmetic, and food companies do battle to define just what the most upscale of the upscale might be. And always, just around the bend, there is tomorrow's "upscale" that makes today's "downscale." The greatest impact of all this by far is the product of the media itself: the fact that it is driven by and generates greater discontent, if not outright unhappiness.[2] We seem to trade on lack of enjoyment. If more is always better, then we never get enough.

There is another way. Rather than trying to achieve certain ends in spite of obstacles or barriers, we might choose to live and share with others. Rather than managing our lives, we could live in community. Rather than thinking we have to produce change, we could adopt those currents that made us happiest. Rather than thinking we have to bring God into situations, we might seek to discern where God is already present. In this context, the shaping power of the church community is more important than ever.

There is a difference between the culture we live in and the church we also live in. God is present and active in both, so this is not a diatribe against culture. But if there is no difference between the church and its culture, then the best we can do is to form smaller communities of enjoyment and resistance—for instance, house churches. However, the wider church cannot give up its role of discerning where and how God is present. God may be present in judgment and in calling for repentance and renewal—for the sake of the abundant life.

The church, the community of Jesus Christ, has an alternative vision. That is my deep-rooted conviction. What is new to me is the realization that the world needs that vision for its own well-being. Christians are called to a new goal—to cultivate a deeper participation in life, which can promote profound enjoyment for us and others. Sometimes we are prone to think of enjoyment as taking us out of our lives, introducing flash, dash, and glamour not essentially our own into our (pathetic) lives. How insulting that premise is! I think of the entertainment or activities I enjoy—movies, racquetball, shopping, going out—and realize that I am seeking a continuous rush of excitement, almost a bodily acceleration. In part this involves an escape from who I am. Once the excitement is over, I start looking for the next rush.

What I want is contentment that comes from following my delights: I want to enjoy my life as it is at present rather than dashing toward the future so hard that the present smacks me in the behind and brings me back to earth. More precisely put, I want to enjoy living my life in the present.

I believe that is probably what most of us want as well—not to give up racquetball or skiing or movies or going out, but enjoying what is, what we do. Food is such a great avenue toward that delight. Honoring our bodies through exercise and taking care of our health is clearly part of that enjoyment. The church offers an indispensable witness and base of support for this.

CHRISTIAN COMMUNITY

Christians affirm that the church is an alternative community—a distinctive community. What does that mean? In what ways does the church claim to be distinctive, especially regarding food practices? Does that path lead to enjoying what is; does it lead to delight? The church affirms that the path of Christ leads not only to delight but also to fulfillment, to salvation. Those claims and questions are the ones we consider in this section.

The act of saying grace, especially before the Eucharist, is to hallow those who gather around the table who share and eat the bread. It is to create a holy (hallowed) people. This act gives our eating a heightened sense of communion with God. We thereby become grateful for God's blessings that come to rest on the gathered community but also overflow them to become blessings for others. These are not just tired theological assertions; they are in fact quite contemporary in their implications for the church, the body of Jesus Christ. They render that community distinctive and offer new hope for eating (and living) in delight.

Christians, of course, confess Jesus to be the bread of life for the whole world. This is true not in an individual-by-individual sense but in the sense that Jesus created a community that follows his example of being concerned for the others' well-being. Monika Hellwig writes that rather than "a vision of innumerable believers all related individually to Jesus, saved and sustained by him by some hidden inner change and acknowledging him in some hidden inner way," in the New Testament "we see a nucleus community that clusters around Jesus and through whom he often works before his death. It is this community which is transformed and becomes the bearer of the new life."[3]

Specifically, Jesus is the bread of life in the concrete and physical sense that the early Christian community, alive in Jesus, was concerned for the needs of others. Those who had received new life felt secure enough not to hoard, not to possess more than others, and not to chase substitute satisfactions such as power, status, privilege, or overconsumption. "Their security rested in the community," Hellwig says.[4] Like them, for us to be nourished by Jesus means to share in his life for others and to be sustained both by the good things of the world—food!—as well as by the Word of God. The early church and ours are built on the foundation of Jesus and the Spirit.

Food as a Communal Expression of Grace

It is anything but coincidental that food and eating, as well as language about eating and metaphors for eating, are so much involved in traditional Christian beliefs. Physical food and eating are absolutely essential to our well-being; furthermore, food is a communal experience. Food is also symbolically important; being nourished and revived are almost always communal acts whereby we are sustained even as we sustain others. Food expresses a relationship; eating together sustains our relationships and regenerates and extends them. It also creates new relationships and reveals that all people are gathered at the table.

Hellwig reminds us that grace is not a substance occasionally meted out by God. Rather, "it is a relationship with God and his creation."[5] The communal frame of relationship enables us to see God's grace in food and eating. Is that food more physical than symbolic, or more symbolic than physical? It is clearly and irrevocably both! The community that still clusters around Jesus through the Holy Spirit recognizes in food the grace of the incarnate one who hungered and thirsted just like us. When we say grace and give thanks, we acknowledge that we are claimed by Jesus and that our community seeks to bear and share new life. We are constituted as a covenant community. Implicit in creation is God's relationship with all humankind and all creation. Only in covenant can we exist, encourage, and support—and be encouraged and supported. Through this covenant we delight, because of this covenant we share. Sharing food is primordial, just as is delight.

These are strong claims about what actually happens in the church. While I find this a powerful—even transforming—vision, I know my own capacity to live out of God's grace depends on a sense of covenant. In those covenant communities, at those times when my sense of communal solidarity is strong, I come closer to living graciously and openly. Then I know that Christ is bread for all peoples and welcomes all to the table equally. My own sense of God's presence is mediated by the visible church community and empowers me to mediate that presence. Much depends on the community of believers. Do we live transformative lives? Do our lives reflect a lifestyle that distinctively bespeaks care for others? Do we live by gift or by grasp? How does this inform our food practices?

By contrast, when I am either out of relationship with the community or when the community is weaker, it is difficult to feel the bonds of the covenant. For me, and for many others, the community birthed by Jesus mediates God's presence. When our relationship is strong, then I can delight and share. When weak, I am more prone to hoard and grasp. To be sure, the strength of this relationship is not the only mediator of God's grace, nor is the relationship to food practices automatic or deterministic.

It is important to note that the covenant community includes the family and subgroups of Christians. It is not limited to the corporate body gathered on Sunday mornings, nor is it only local. The local body, whether family or interpersonal or small group, is very significant. The extended, global *communio* and the communion of the saints are extensions of the local and historic covenant communities whose impact is less directly and proximately influential, but whose significance is real and awaits rediscovery.[6]

This hunger to be fulfilled is ongoing, and it is not limited to Christians. The need to be in communion with others, so evident when we eat together, knows no ideological or religious boundaries. When our hunger is not satisfied, we human beings tend to engage in destructive behavior. Our hunger to love and be loved, when stymied, produces depression or violence against others. We all yearn to be saved. God calls us all to be reunited, redirected in a Godward way. The call to delight and share is issued to all eaters; it takes distinctive shape for those who understand that God is the master gardener and the ultimate cook.

The Visionary Church

There are several forms that the church's outreach, its sharing, can take. This is what I was referring to when I spoke earlier of God's blessings overflowing the Christian community so that they could become blessings for others. Here I point to four dimensions of sharing.

Continuous Conversion

In order to share, the church must first itself be continuously converted. This is always risky, for it calls us to trust both that God loves us and that we can trust the community of Jesus enough to invest in it. The process of redemption is never fully achieved. In fact, our own conversion to trusting, delighting, and sharing is in process as long as we live. We continue to become aware of the dimensions of the food system and acknowledge our individual and corporate (especially corporate) roles in it. The church and its members are also actively transforming the system and alleviating the hunger and suffering it produces.

This is not a matter of the church getting its act straight before it articulates a vision, the second form of outreach we mention here. We cannot wait that long! Indeed, the church's ongoing conversion is an act of witness which itself depends on having a vision. Realistically the church must struggle to embody that vision more and more. Part of that vision is a distinctive way of understanding what food is. Indeed, this whole book could be seen as just such an articulation.

The East Lake Andes Lutheran Church in South Dakota has a practice that I very much commend to other churches. Every Sunday they have a potluck meal together after worship. It is hard to remain conflicted with someone you eat with every week. Fellowship and mutual caring develop. Ongoing conversion and formation can happen. As a matter of fact, this was the practice at my boyhood church—the Plains Presbyterian Church in Zachary, Louisiana. In light of these suggestions, weekly celebration or Eucharist also makes sense.

Re-envisioning a Different Model

If the first process involves our continuous conversion, the second is to re-envision, to re-think what we as church need to be about. This begins with a fairly cognitive, reflection-oriented process.

Theologian Sallie McFague offers one version of the "task of Christian churches at the beginning of the millennium," which are "faced . . . with a global society characterized by a notion of abundance that is in direct opposition to divine abundance—a notion of abundance that is impoverishing and devastating 'God's body.'"[7] McFague thinks this involves saying no to capitalism and its consumerism, which is especially pernicious because it is so interwoven into cultures of affluence and can be so devastating to ecological and rural community life support systems. The church's role is to teach and live out a different view of the abundant life that is "aligned with the ecological economic model."[8]

The paradigm McFague sketches is one that lives with a priority for justice and living in a caring way. She writes that we "must individually and collectively devise alternative ways of working, eating, cultivating land, transporting ourselves, educating our children, entertaining ourselves, even of worshiping God."[9] Part of that revolution in practices is happening as people rediscover gardening, cooking, sharing child raising, home schooling, and other means of local interdependency.

MORAL DELIBERATION

Concomitantly the church is called to study the Word of God, to deliberate on its moral stances, to advocate for the maximum possible degree of justice, and to proclaim the truth of God's purposes. These tasks of political advocacy and firm resistance to evil accompany strong proclamation. They are, in fact, proclamation. The Word of God as it is preached in local pulpits is also the word that needs to be discerned in the world as well as discussed in the pew. The re-envisionment about which McFague speaks must be proclaimed, witnessed, and lived out.

This vision is an economic one as well. The individual efforts of Christians to live responsibly and enjoyably deserve the support of the community. Investing in efforts to grow healthy food in ways that sustain local farmers, communities, and the land make good sense for all of us. Calling corporations to responsible action and working with them toward ensuring a safe and healthy diet for people and planet is a foundational way for the church to witness. We cannot afford the luxury of carping at big bad corporations from places of presumed purity. We in the church need both to offer an alternate vision for mega-corporations and to live out that vision locally.

David Korten, in his *Post-Corporate World: Life after Capitalism,* offers an economic and social perspective that moves beyond an us-against-them corporation mentality.[10] He suggests that many of the unsustainable burdens we place on our planet result from choices that not only deprive others of some of the most basic means of living, they also diminish the lives of us all, often for the purpose of increasing corporate profits. His alternative is to begin to focus on our local places, their economics and politics. His best advice may be the answer he gives to the question, What can I do? He answers, "Start from where you are."[11] Begin with your personal buying habits, at your job, in the capacities you have, in your neighborhood, in your church.

There is a vast network of local resources available to combat the most pernicious effects of industrial and commercial globalization; these might be captured under the term *localization.* The localization he commends stays in conversation and cooperates with other local and global movements to avoid provincialism. Nevertheless, it is unwilling to capitulate to hegemonic powers that take local decisions and local cultural values out of the hands of community residents. Community-supported agriculture, housing arrangements that collaboratively buy and use machinery, community gardens, municipal politics, neighborhood watches—all these and innumerable others are ways of starting where we are.

LIVING THE VISION

Furthermore, the church needs to attend to the salvation of the affluent, ourselves included. The path toward our salvation is exactly the same that Jesus urged upon the rich young ruler; we must learn to share. The affluent need salvation as much, if not more, than others; we *need* to surrender what is "ours," to take risks, to stop hoarding, to live in community. How we are to do this in a way that best loves the neighbor is not clear; make no mistake, however, Jesus calls us to do it *for ourselves.* That is the path toward *our* fulfillment. We can do this because we experience the challenging and affirming love of Christ in the community of Eucharist. As we more and more learn the fullness that comes with sharing our life, the more we know that losing one's self is to find one's self in Christ.

Monika Hellwig's finest words in *The Eucharist and the Hunger of the World* are these: "In the Eucharist we have an answer to despair about the future of the world; we can still live and bid others live because we are drawn into a covenant with God and all [hu]mankind within which to give one's life for others is ultimately to save one's life."[12]

That is the way to put the hungry ghosts in one's life to rest. We can begin doing this simply. We begin with practices that shape us as we participate in them. We do best when we practice in church and community. Practices surrounding food and eating are one of the best avenues for building upon Christ's injunctions. We can all understand hunger, because we all eat every day. Food makes a direct connection between our beliefs and our daily life. Eating is a practical, easily comprehended, foundational experience. Developing such practices is easy to do; it is a daily routine, and it helps avoid the segregation of religious matters to an isolated sector of life. It encourages a spirituality that is not ethereal or fragmented but pervasive, concrete, and holistic. Furthermore, the Christian faith is replete with practices connected to food.

We could include here a long list of activities that encourage the appreciation of food and the alleviation of others' (as well as our own) hunger. However tempting it may be to produce just such a list of "things to do," I want to limit this to three core practices:

1. Pray carefully in church and at home. Say grace before meals thoughtfully in a way that recognizes the specifics of the meal and of what is going on in your life. Being specific about what all goes into getting food prepared and on the table helps us not only be aware of this blessing, it also puts us in relationship with God. It helps us recognize that we live in grace.

2. Find a way of sharing food with others, especially others who cannot share in return. Do this for yourself, for Christ's sake! Some good ways to do this are by volunteering regularly in a soup kitchen or working in a food pantry or helping to staff a shelter for homeless or otherwise disadvantaged persons. You

could begin in small ways to share with those, like children or the elderly or shut-ins, who need food to be provided. At the least we can make certain food is provided through such agencies as the Christian Children's Fund or Heifer Project International. Sharing face-to-face is better. Get to know individual people. Prepare the meal yourself.

3. Make it a practice to know where your food comes from and to eat as locally as possible. This may mean growing *some* of your own food and appreciating what comes close to home. Seek to discover where God is active in your local food supply system. Where does food waste go? Learning about the source of your food and eating (and buying) locally will be a great joy and it will also be a spiritual blessing to expect to find God at work in all the processes that produce food and delight at table. You will not be far from worship at that point.

Food and Public Ministry

Psychologist Carl G. Jung wrote that "Bidden or not bidden, God is present."[13] This reminds us Christians that God is active in the world, sustaining and redeeming. We talk of Jesus as the life of the world and conceive of the Holy Spirit as dynamically working through the church but also quite independently of the church. It is also clear that God loves the whole world and all the species in it. Those who profess faith in the Triune God are called to love God and all neighbors. Thus the church exists for the whole world, and not only to enrich its own internal life. Indeed, when the whole body is working properly, the church is in mission to the world. It not only has a public ministry, it is founded on a commission to go out into all the world (Matt. 28:19-20), and it exists for public ministry.

When we think of this mission and ministry to the whole world in terms of food and the global food system, then we can assert that the church is to carry out God's dual purposes for food and eating: delight and sharing. A quite obvious mandate for the church is to put an end to world hunger and malnutrition. In chapter 5, I called world hunger the most extreme disorder; the "social program" virtually all churches and most nations can agree to combat is the pariah of world hunger. This is probably because we can imagine the pain of destructive hunger, because the pain of hunger or injury pushes other necessities of life to the background until these are satisfied. The malnutrition we are thinking of is that of *under*nourishment, even though *over*nourishment is—as we have seen—a problem as well.

Hunger is related to racism, to wars of ethnic cleansing, and to health care. All of these are related to economics and to the gap between rich and poor. When the church begins to address this primary material and spiritual issue, it begins to encounter great resistance. The thread of hunger takes us to the warp and woof of economic and political life. We do not want to have our drive for economic security and well-being pitted against our faith in God. We want to see these two as being capable of living together in great comfort.

Much of Jesus' ministry addressed the hungry and the sick. Perhaps it is Jesus' egalitarianism (and his lack of a visible settled means of support with a pension plan) that most bothers us. John Dominic Crossan, a New Testament scholar, writes that the open table fellowship and "radical egalitarianism of Jesus' kingdom of God are more terrifying than anything we have ever imagined, and even if we can never accept it, we should not explain it away as something else."[14] The radical abundance of the Lord's open table terrifies us, for it calls us to share and finally to trust God for our daily bread.

Thus far we have been able to see God's provision of daily bread only as a backup plan in case our own comfortable livelihood were to fail. Sallie McFague is even more emphatic: "For us well-off Christians, sin is not principally personal or sexual; rather, it is our refusal to acknowledge our terror at the prospect of the systemic economic changes needed for the just and sustainable distribution of the world's goods to all people and other creatures. *That* is truly terrifying for us."[15] McFague invites us to a "wild space," a perspective beyond the majority position from which we can see differently. "That wild space is the shocking suggestion—even if only a suspicion—that *all* really are invited to the banquet, that every creature deserves a place at the table."[16] Indeed, this is similar to the vision of the Messianic banquet of Isaiah 25 or of Luke 14:15-24.

The reason why the "economic changes needed to produce a just and sustainable place at the table for everyone" terrify us is because we have been hogging more than our share. We might have to give up the crème caramel or the panacotta. We would have to stop protecting our overshare. We would have to stop consuming too much. For that to happen, we would have to trust God's abundance and other people. We might be able to give up our complicity. Our food might begin to taste better. We might begin to stop being overnourished. We could begin to delight in our own and in our neighbor's bodily well-being.

It is thinkable that we could enjoy sharing, if we are correct that delight and sharing proceed in lockstep, however incrementally. We could delight in the more abundant life for all. We would not have to ignore the way our gluttony takes food off of someone else's plate. Instead, we could see others as dinner companions. Wouldn't it be wonderful if our virtues were enjoyable and that we could delight in table fellowship with all beings? I believe that is what God intends and where we find our maximum enjoyment, but I do not think we are there yet.

How do we get there? What is the church's—and the society's— public ministry? There are a number of things that are necessary:

- A concern for the health of the soil and water and air quality needed to grow healthy food in an ongoing way;
- Equitable prices for farmers and for those communities that are committed to growing healthy food and renewing the health of the planet;
- A commitment to developing a supply system of local foods in a way that feeds local peoples throughout the globe to the maximum degree possible;
- Justice for those who are workers in food industries, which includes an income adequate for a good life;
- Public policies that encourage business corporations and political entities to invest in disadvantaged countries and communities in long-term, cumulative, and food secure ways;[17]
- Protection from environmental dumping and other dangerous practices for disadvantaged groups and those without the power to oppose them;

- Public promotion of healthy foods and a vigorous lifestyle that maximizes opportunities for enjoyable physical activities and delightful eating; and
- World trade policies, built on sustainable sufficiency for all, which are tilted toward increasing the joy that God intended for all creatures.

All these and other steps can be tailored to particular contexts and churches. What is essential is to begin.

There are multiple steps that the church can take and can urge its denomination, government, and corporate offices to take toward these ends: supporting Bread for the World, denominational hunger programs, Church World Service, Catholic Relief Agencies; working for more equitable legislation; teaching our children that hunger is an abomination; and promoting systems that allow people to sustain themselves rather than grow crops to feed others who cannot afford them. These are vital steps. But the bottom line is that it begins with you and me.

Delight and share!

Notes

PREFACE

1. David Leonhardt, "If Richer Isn't Happier, What Is?" *New York Times* (May 19, 2001), B9.

2. Richard M. Fewkes, "The Theology of Eating" (sermon, First Parish Unitarian, Norwell, Mass., March 22, 1998) http://www.gis.net/~fpnma/sermons/eating.htm.

1. HUNGRY FOR MORE

1. *The Westminster Shorter Catechism*, answer to question 1; "What is man's chief end?"

2. This phrase, though not terribly elegant, is immensely helpful to me. Thanks to Jay McDaniel and John L. Farthing, "John Wesley, Process Theology, and Consumerism," in *Thy Nature and Thy Name Is Love*, ed. Bryan P. Stone and Thomas Jay Oord (Norman, Okla.: Kingswood, 2001), 355–77.

3. See Arlie Hochschild, *The Time Bind: When Work Becomes Home and Home Becomes Work* (New York: Holt, 2001), and also, Arlie Hochschild and Anne Machung, *Second Shift: Working Parents and the Revolution at Home* (New York: Vintage, 1989), on the amount that Americans overwork.

4. See Claudia Janssen, "Bodily Resurrection (1 Cor. 15)? The Discussion of Resurrection in Karl Barth, Rudolf Bultmann, Dorothee Soelle and Contemporary Feminist Theology," *Journal for the Study of the New Testament* 79 (September 2000): 61–78. Janssen shows that many feminist theologians view resurrection as an experience of God's activity today. Resurrection is located in the everyday life of women and men in the New Testament age and in the present. It is a collective event that lifts up the value of our

bodily, material life as well as our responsibility in the world. Janssen calls the church to be the empowering center where resurrection is to be preached, practiced personally, and lifted up as the public goal of the Christian life. We are to *be* bodily resurrection in the church.

The strong emphasis on experience in contemporary theology does not eradicate the place of cognition. As John Dewey wrote, "Reflection is natural and continuous." Experience is always more or less reflective. It gives rise to, indeed almost demands, reflection. Furthermore, we struggle to interpret our complex and also seemingly inconsistent experiences—even religious experiences—through more or less rational reflection. However, in light of theology's proclivity toward cognitive abstraction, it is important to recall the primacy of experience, especially for this project.

5. Quoted by Monika Hellwig, *The Eucharist and the Hunger of the World*, 2nd ed. (Franklin, Wis.: Sheed & Ward, 1999), vii. Hellwig uses Gadamer's example to make the point that words—theological formulations—are intended to pass along on the third level the meaning of the experience on the first. We know that words cannot capture fully the reality of experience either in the Lord's Supper or in the everyday experience of eating.

6. Theologian Sallie McFague's reasons for emphasizing the primacy of experience are pertinent to the present task. She claims, "The purpose of theology is to glorify God by reflecting on how we might live better on earth. Theology is about thinking, but it is not primarily an intellectual activity. It is a practical one—so that we might live better, more appropriately, in the world." See Sallie McFague, *Life Abundant: Rethinking Theology and Economy for a Planet in Peril* (Minneapolis: Fortress Press, 2001), 25. McFague by no means denigrates the work of the intellect for the sake of living in a way that is morally appropriate; indeed, for her, the intellectual is in the service of the moral life. However, she is quite clear that the quality of the experience we live has first priority.

The faith foundations of McFague's theology are also, interestingly, more conspicuous and influential in this book than in her previous ones. Confirming this priority are arguments on 31–33, 64–65, 89, 102–3, 137, and 186–88.

7. Douglas John Hall, a major Canadian theologian, makes a great deal of our North American "official religion of optimism," which avoids the negations of life—divorce, drug addiction, pain and suffering, and ultimately death. This avoidance, born of an inability to accept or interpret or—dare I say—appreciate such negations, renders them terrifying gaps, which we have simply not been able to control completely. There is a great cost attached to this official, but clearly non-Christian religion. It is particularly difficult to maintain this religion in the wake of the events of September 11, 2001, but I do believe that some of the reactions to those events were illustrative of the myopic optimism we Americans exhibit.

There is also a magnitude of grace involved in proclaiming—in Claudia Janssen's way—the gospel of bodily resurrection in such a culture. See Douglas John Hall, "Courage to Change . . . the Church!" a series of three lectures given at Lutheran Theological School in Chicago that encapsulates much of Hall's trilogy on thinking, professing, and confessing the faith. *Currents in Theology and Mission* 22:6 (December 1995).

8. I am indebted to Monika Hellwig's *The Eucharist and the Hunger of the World* for her description of the wider "hungers" human beings experience, especially her work on pages 1–20. Hers is a truly remarkable piece of work. On the way in which pain of any type begins to expand and take over other aspects of life, see Elaine Scarry, *The Body in Pain: The Making and Unmaking of the World* (New York: Oxford University Press, 1985).

9. At this point, it is vital to mention, at least, how integrally the social location and context of the writer and reader enter into this brief sketch. The hunger of the "search for meaning" of the well fed is quite different from the hunger of the physically starving, which is an obsessive craving for food that erodes social and moral and any other kinds of constraints.

I have been struck by the selflessness of mothers who are themselves starving for their dying children. I realize that this is the exception that proves the rule: it is the strength of the drive to avoid starvation that makes such selflessness remarkable.

This book sometimes refers to God in female terms. Though in all cases, either gender is appropriate, sometimes seeing God as female evokes richer associations than referring to God as male, especially in matters of cooking and caring. Maybe this is because my grandmother was both a great cook and an unconditional grandson-lover.

10. Leon Kass, *The Hungry Soul: Eating and the Perfecting of our Nature* (Chicago: University of Chicago Press, 1994), 48. Kass's is a perceptive philosophical account of the way eating informs and constitutes human nature. On the way the cognitive is permeated by the visceral, see, among others, Diane Fritz Cates, *Choosing to Feel: Virtue, Friendship, and Compassion for Friends* (Notre Dame, Ind.: Notre Dame University Press, 1997). One especially helpful, now older book is that by James B. Nelson, *Embodiment: An Approach to Sexuality and Christian Theology* (Minneapolis: Augsburg, 1978).

11. Kass, *Hungry Soul*, xv.

12. Ibid., 27.

13. Ibid., 22.

14. Michelle Lelwica, *Starving for Salvation: The Spiritual Dimensions of Eating Problems among American Girls and Women* (New York: Oxford University Press, 1999).

15. Hellwig, *Eucharist and Hunger*, 9.

16. Ibid., 13

2. GOD'S INTENTION FOR FOOD

1. See Howard Harrod's article, "Interpreting and Projecting: Two Elements of the Self as Moral Agent," *Journal of the American Academy of Religion* 41 (March 1973): 18–29, regarding the way Jesus Christ enters into the routine cognitive and psychological dynamics of the moral life.

Alfred Schutz maintains that it is natural to "typify" a person or event or place or food after one has left the immediate experience of that person, event, place, or food. This is the way that we carry around an image of that entity for future reference. It is what we are doing when we remember that entity.

2. It makes a great deal of difference theologically whether one speaks of the will or purpose of God, or of the presence of God. At this point, however, there is no need to differentiate between them. I have internalized two books by Larry Rasmussen and Bruce Birch in regard to how Scripture relates to Christian ethics—*The Bible and Ethics in the Christian Life* (Minneapolis: Augsburg, 1976) and *The Predicament of the Prosperous* (Philadelphia: Westminster, 1978), respectively. These are still the best two books I know relating ethics and Scripture. Much of what follows depends on principles enunciated in them.

3. Scripture can even judge itself; this becomes particularly evident when we become aware of our inadequate, limited, or wrong past interpretations of Scripture. For example, the feminist movement has used Scripture to judge the adequacy of patriarchal structures, which were simply assumed in biblical times and which at least devalued and often oppressed women. I think of the work of Letty Russell, Phyllis Trible, and Elisabeth Schüssler Fiorenza in this regard.

Scripture portrays God as calling us to righteousness, but also as loving and forgiving us. Thus are we enabled to hear words of judgment as ultimately gracious. One evidence of that is how previously male-dominated churches have recognized the inequities of the past and included women as equal partners and leaders. Far from suffering, many churches with women in leadership roles are thriving like never before.

The recognition of sin and evil is made possible by the assurance of grace. This becomes important to our project here because beginning with experience can result in the muting of the prophetic voice in Scripture. We can wind up simply saying that God endorses gourmet dining. However, Scripture itself is experiential and calls us to pay attention to the destructive forces of injustice and evil. Scripture calls us to the misappropriation of material goods and privileges, to care for those who are disadvantaged—the poor, victims of injustice, those who cannot help themselves. Sometimes Scripture points to the need for the prophetic voice of an Amos or a Hosea or a Jesus. My thanks go to Dr. Cheryl Anderson of Garrett Evangelical Theological Seminary for pushing me on this point.

Scripture is a living document, of course, or should be. It is no more self-sufficient to produce revelation than any other historical document. Christians claim, however, that Scripture trains them in discernment and expectation, not to mention other moral virtues.

4. Miroslav Volf, "Theology for a Way of Life," in *Practicing Theology: Beliefs and Practices in the Christian Life*, ed. Miroslav Volf and Dorothy Bass (Grand Rapids: Eerdmans, 2001), 252–53.

5. There are elements of the covenant implicit in this creation story; human beings are gifted and given mandates for their actions. Similarly, in the second creation story (Gen. 2:4b-25) the Lord God plants a garden in Eden and puts men and women there to till it and to keep it.

6. Walter Brueggemann, *Genesis*, Interpretation: The Bible Commentary for Teaching and Preaching series (Atlanta: John Knox, 1982), 39. Quoted by Sara Covin Juengst, *Breaking Bread: The Spiritual Significance of Food* (Louisville: Westminster John Knox, 1992), 24.

7. Claus Westermann, *Blessing in the Bible and in the Life of the Church.* (Philadelphia: Fortress Press, 1978).

8. Douglas M. Meeks, *God the Economist: The Doctrine of God and Political Economy* (Minneapolis: Fortress Press, 1989), and Walter Brueggemann, "The Liturgy of Abundance, the Myth of Scarcity," *Christian Century*, March 24–31, 1999, 342–47.

9. Juengst, *Breaking Bread*, 29.

10. Calvin speaks of eating to the glory of God in a way that exemplifies the response of stewardship: "We must take care that, even in eating and drinking, we may aim at the advancement of [God's glory]. . . . It was well expressed in a common proverb, that we must not live to eat, but eat to live. Provided that the end of living be at the same time kept in view, the consequences will thus be, that our food will be in a manner sacred to God, inasmuch as it will be set apart for his service" (John Calvin, *Commentary on the First Epistle to the Corinthians* [Grand Rapids: Eerdmans, 1948 (orig. pub. 1546)], 347).

11. Philip J. King, "Commensality in the Bible," in *Hesed Vo-Emet: Studies in Honor of Ernest S. Frerichs*, ed. Jodi Magness and Seymour Gitin (Atlanta: Scholars Press, 1998), 53.

12. Juengst, *Breaking Bread*, 42 and all of chapter 3, "Hospitality: Expression of Grace," 37–47. Juengst's whole book is a compendium of biblical sources on food.

13. Leon R. Kass, *The Hungry Soul: Eating and the Perfecting of Our Nature* (Chicago: University of Chicago Press, 1994). See chapter 6.

14. Ibid., 231. The sanctification toward which Kass points is reminiscent of Calvin's direction that our eating is sacred if it is done to the glory of God and set apart to God's service and glory (see note 10). Both see eating as an occasion for human sanctification. (Note, however, that Kass is not linking sanctification to Jesus Christ.)

15. Sara Juengst reminds us that Søren Kierkegaard interpreted this passage as indicating that food, drink, and clothing are good to the extent they

support our relationship with God. When we recognize these good things as God's gifts, then we can live in trust that God will supply what we need. Having confidence in God, trusting God, breaks our anxiety. We learn to trust; that shapes our lives. *Breaking Bread*, 25.

16. The literature on the origins and meaning of the institution of the Lord's Supper is vast. See John Koenig, *The Feast of the World's Redemption: Eucharistic Origins and Christian Mission* (Harrisburg, Pa.: Trinity Press International, 2000), especially chapters 4 and 5. I appreciate Koenig's balanced treatment and his view of the New Testament as a document for the church in the present.

17. Ibid., 61. This anticipation of the kingdom also explains why Paul was so angry about the way the Corinthian Christians were practicing (or not practicing!) communion.

18. World Council of Churches, *Baptism, Eucharist, and Ministry*, 1982, Eucharist II, sec. D and E, 14–15.

19. Apparently in the early church there was a more sustained and even boisterous meal that accompanied worship. Sometimes it apparently even got wild!

20. See Juengst, *Breaking Bread*, 76–87 passim.

21. See Sallie McFague, *Models of God: Theology for an Ecological, Nuclear Age* (Philadelphia: Fortress Press, 1987), especially chapter 6.

22. Marianne Sawicki, "Recognizing the Risen Lord," *Theology Today* 44 (January 1988), 449.

23. Koenig, *Feast of the World's Redemption*, xiii. Koenig cites classic works that point to "the missionary quality of the New Testament meals." See also Alexander Schmemann, *For the Life of the World* (Geneva: WCC, 1963); J.G. Davies, *Worship and Mission* (London: SCM, 1966); and Geoffrey Wainwright, *Eucharist and Eschatology* (New York: Oxford, 1971).

24. Koenig, *Feast of the World's Redemption*, 82–85.

3. FOOD AND THE CHRISTIAN EXPERIENCE

1. For example, in Peter L. Berger's *Rumor of Angels: Modern Society and the Rediscovery of the Supernatural* (New York: Doubleday, 1969), he suggests that the feeling of moral revulsion can itself be a rumor, an experience whose negative force reveals what is morally to be strived for. However, one might also say that noticing, taking care, feeling compassion, and addressing the situation of the homeless are actions that do bring satisfaction and a deep sense of fulfillment. Even then, however, the point stands: the satisfaction or fulfillment is not a sufficient guide to action.

2. Sallie McFague, *Life Abundant: Rethinking Theology and Economy for a Planet in Peril* (Minneapolis: Fortress Press, 2001), xii–xiii.

3. Ibid., 54.

4. Ibid., 55.

5. Despite the primary focus of this work—*eating*—it is important to keep another eye open to *food*. With eating, one can begin to ignore exactly what is being eaten; the human act threatens to dissolve the otherness of the animals and plants that are being consumed. Thus can vanish a concern for ecological health, world trade, the ethical treatment of animals, practices of food preparation, and those who labor in the food supply industry. Furthermore, such a focus on eating can threaten to disguise the centrality of the human body and the way food safety can interact with human health. See Stephen H. Webb, *Good Eating* (Waco, Tex.: Brazos, 2001).

6. "In 2000, USDA issued a food recall once every five days. In 2001, recalls occurred once every four days. In 2002, recalls occurred once every three days. . . . USDA confessed that nearly 60 percent of the largest U.S. meat plants inspected last fall flunked federal E. coli food-safety regulations." Alan Guebert, "New USDA Budget Filled with Political Puffery, Numerical Quackery," *Dubuque* (Iowa) *Telegraph Herald* (February 9, 2003).

7. See Gordon D. Kaufman, "Reconceiving God and Humanity in Light of Today's Ecological Consciousness: A Brief Statement," *Cross Currents* 50, vols. 1 and 2 (spring/summer 2000) and "Problem for Theology: The Concept of Nature," *Harvard Theological Review* 65 (July 1972): 337–66. "An unspoken presupposition . . . throughout much Christian history has been that faith and theology are concerned basically with what we today call the existential issues of life—despair, guilt, death, meaningfulness, anxiety, sin, and so on, the problems that arise because we are self-conscious subjects and agents. God's love, mercy, forgiveness, justification by faith were said to address these issues of finitude and sinfulness, and enable life to go on. This sort of focus and imagery, I suggest, encourages an understanding of both the Christian God and Christian faith in fundamentally human-centered terms, and as bearing largely on certain personal problems."

8. Gordon D. Kaufman, "Reconceiving God and Humanity," 103–4.

9. Ibid., 105–7.

10. See Douglas John Hall, "Courage to Change . . . the Church!" *Currents in Theology and Mission* 22:6 (December 1995), passim, but especially 409, 410. Hall makes much of the fact that we have created quite sophisticated ways of avoiding the acknowledgment of mortality and death.

11. Two places where I examine this rootage in depth are *We Are Home: A Spirituality of the Environment* (Mahwah, N.J.: Paulist, 1993), chap. 2; also "The Ethics of Agriculture and the Material World," *Annual of the Society of Christian Ethics*, 1986 (Washington D.C.: Georgetown University Press, 1987), 219–42. Generally speaking, neo-orthodox theology, Kantian ethics, and Cartesian philosophy bear responsibility for ignoring the impact of our material physical constitution upon holistic thinking and action. The anthropological assumptions of these movements were faulty and dangerous.

12. Marcus Barth, *Rediscovering the Lord's Supper: Communion with Israel, with Christ, and Among the Guests* (Atlanta: John Knox, 1988), 1.

13. Origen, *De princ.* 1.7, quoted in Justo L. González, *Christian Thought Revisited: Three Types of Theology*, rev. ed. (Maryknoll, N.Y.: Orbis, 1999), 26. González's typology is helpful, as is his three-volume *A History of Christian Thought* (Nashville: Abingdon, 1970–1975).

14. This is, incidentally, the model that has generated my own Reformed tradition, which exhibits both the assets and the liabilities of the Alexandrine tradition.

15. Irenaeus, *Adv. Haer.*, 4, prol. (ANF, 1:463), from Justo González, *History of Christian Thought*, 28.

16. Ibid., 41.

17. There is no essential inconsistency between the Alexandrine and Antiochene. Indeed, there are real assets to the Alexandrine that will prove vital. The liability of the Antiochene is that it does not foster an ability to make distinctions and use the Spirit-filled gift of human reasoning for political and economic ends to the extent that the Alexandrine does.

18. Tertullian, *Adv. Herm.* 36.4, Quoted by Douglas Burton-Christie, *Weavings* (July–August 1999): 45.

19. This has considerable implications for the way in which the church does ministry. We will tease out some of those in chap. 7.

20. Nancy Fahnholz, "Food Is Love," unpublished paper, Lutheran School of Theology at Chicago (July 2000).

21. See Garret Keizer, "Natural Resistance," *Christian Century* (December 13, 2000), 1302.

22. Robert F. Capron, *The Supper of the Lamb* (New York: Harcourt, Brace, 1967), 40.

23. On the way that our embodiment establishes the fact of our sociality with other women and men, see my "Spatiality, Relativity, and Authority," *Journal of the American Academy of Religion* 50 (June 1982): 215–35. At the lowest level, the fact that our body will encounter resistance if we walk into another (self-conscious) body calls the fact of sociality to mind.

24. Serene Jones, "Graced Practices: Excellence and Freedom in the Christian," in *Theology: Beliefs and Practices in Christian Life*, ed. Miroslav Volf and Dorothy C. Bass (Grand Rapids: Eerdmans, 2002), 60.

4. GOD AND EATING DISORDERS

1. Associated Press, "Experts Say We're Getting Fat," Newscape (Internet), January 30, 2001. Greg Critser reports that "60 percent of Americans are overweight" in *Fat Land: How Americans Became the Fattest People in the World* (Boston: Houghton Mifflin, 2003). There would be a similar tone about any report from the past five years.

2. United Nations, *Human Development Report 1998* (New York: Oxford University Press, 1998).

3. Donald Altman, *Art of the Inner Meal: Eating as a Spiritual Path* (San Francisco: Harper, 1999), 158–60,165. It should be noted that this image shares any number of anthropological implications with the theology of Augustine, Thomas Aquinas, Martin Luther, H. Richard Niebuhr, and Aristotle.

4. Michelle Mary Lelwica, *Starving for Salvation: The Spiritual Dimensions of Eating Problems among American Girls and Women* (New York: Oxford University Press, 1999), 37, 38.

5. Erica Goode, "Seeking New Clues to Eating Disorders," *International Herald Tribune* (October 26, 2000), 10.

6. Center for Science in the Public Interest, "The Pressure to Eat: Why We're Getting Fatter," *Nutrition Action Healthletter* (July/August 1998), www.cspinet.org. Dr. Brownell is Professor of Psychology, Epidemiology, and Public Health at Yale University.

7. Ibid.

8. Mary Sykes Wylie, "Our Trip to Bountiful," *The Family Therapy Networker* (May/June 1997), 25. As evidence of this, she cites conflicting food rules, official pronouncements, collective food angst, and pop diets.

9. Interestingly, the prescription for obesity that *Fat Land* makes—after having documented the ways that cultural institutions encourage obesity— is to encourage greater individual self-control. My analysis suggests far deeper roots and more profound social surgery.

10. Wylie, "Trip to Bountiful," 31.

11. Quoted in ibid., 29.

12. See Mary Pipher, *Reviving Ophelia: Saving the Selves of Adolescent Girls* (New York: Ballantine, 1995), and Joan Jacobs Brumberg, *The Body Project: An Intimate History of American Girls* (New York: Random House, 1997). For boys see Harrison G. Pope Jr., Katharine Phillips, and Roberto Olivardia, *The Adonis Complex: The Secret Crisis of Male Body Obsession* (New York: Free Press, 2000).

13. There may be some foreshadowing of forgiveness in this sequencing.

14. Lelwica, *Starving for Salvation*, chapter 1.

15. Jane E. Brody, "Private Hell of Eating Disorders," *International Herald Tribune* (December 14, 2000), 14.

16. Margaret Bullitt-Jonas, *Holy Hunger: A Memoir of Desire* (New York: Knopf, 1999).

17. Ibid., 62.

18. Ibid., 63, 65.

19. Sin itself can be divided in several ways. A Roman Catholic division understands sin as objective—that is, there are real world actualities that are the result of sin, such as murder or starvation; and also as subjective—as the distortion of our attitudes and misdirection of our actions such as envy or greed or hatred. There may be mitigating or aggravating circumstances for our subjective sin. A more Protestant rendition makes a division between sin and guilt: sin is all those actions and attitudes that are contrary to the will of

God; guilt is the degree to which we are culpable for our sin. Injustice is both sinful and, to some extent, culpable, especially if we are aware of our sinfulness and still choose to practice sin. There are clear overlaps here.

20. Thomas Aquinas, *Summa Theologica* II/1, q. 72, a. 4, quoted by Ted Peters, *Sin: Radical Evil in Self and Society* (Grand Rapids: Eerdmans, 1994), 11. Protestants speak of "sin" as the conglomerate rebellion against God, which is true of all "sins" defined as individual acts of pride or sloth against self and neighbor as well as God.

21. Ibid., 11–20.

22. This is where Reinhold Niebuhr locates the origin of sin as well—in the anxiety of human beings as simultaneously creature and creator. As will become important in this section, it is fascinating that Niebuhr identified two kinds of sin: the outgrowth of both hubris and sensuality, a dimension of sloth. He seems to identify sensuality and sloth, a Protestant mistake in my view. See *The Nature and Destiny of Man*, vol. 1 (New York: Scribners, 1941), 228–40. Niebuhr seems to miss the nuance of sin as self-loathing or underestimation.

23. It is interesting that Jürgen Moltmann doesn't see this as much a matter of lack of faith or trust as a matter of lack of hope or hopelessness; the two seem inseparably linked.

24. The complexities revealed by my analysis of concupiscence and desire cry out for additional study. Protestants (like Peters) have tended to identify concupiscence with disordered desire; for Thomas Aquinas and Roman Catholics, concupiscence is not necessarily disordered. See n. 27 below.

25. Peters, *Sin*, 124–34.

26. See Bullitt-Jones, *Holy Hunger*, 62–70, 109–40.

27. Karl Rahner, "Der theologische Begriff der Konkupiszenz," in *Schriften zur Theologie*, vol. 1, 7th ed. (Einsiedeln, 1964), 347.

28. There has been a far more negative appraisal of concupiscence from a Protestant than Catholic viewpoint. See, for example, Michael Figura, "Concupiscence and Desire from the Point of View of Theological Anthropology," *Communio* 27 (spring 2000): 3–13.

5. Global Food Disorder

1. Craig L. Nessan, *Give Us This Day: A Lutheran Response to World Hunger* (Minneapolis: Fortress Press, 2003). See also James M. Childs Jr., *Greed: Economics and Ethics in Conflict* (Minneapolis: Fortress Press, 2000), especially chap. 5.

2. Quoted in Emmanuel Levinas, *Totality and Infinity* (Pittsburgh: Duquesne University Press, 1969), 201.

3. These figures come from Bread for the World. See David Beckmann and Arthur Simon, *Grace at the Table: Ending Hunger in God's World* (New York: Paulist, 1999),15. There are other estimates of hunger that put the figure at

1.2 billion. A UN website lists 840 million starving worldwide and 34,000 children under the age of five dying every day. See United Nations, "Lecture on the Food Problem," Japan (April 16, 2003), http://www.unic.or.jp/ poverty /03food/01foo.htm.

4. This same list was published in the *Globe and Mail* (Toronto) (July 26, 1999), A13.

5. See Beckmann and Simon, *Grace at the Table,* 66.

6. "Twenty years ago the ratio of average income in the least developed countries to income in the rich world was 1-to-87. Now it is 1-to-98." Kevin Watkins, "More Hot Air Won't Bring the World's Poor in from the Cold," *International Herald Tribune* (May 16, 2001), 8.

7. Ibid.

8. Pontifical Council for Justice and Peace, "Towards A Better Distribution of Land: The Challenge of Agrarian Reform," Libereria Editrice Vaticana, 00120 Citta Del Vaticano, 16.

9. See Mary Hendrickson and William Heffernan, "Concentration of Agricultural Markets" (February 2002), http://www.foodcircles.missouri.edu.

10. David C. Korten, "Institutional Choices for the Third Millennium: Will Corporations Continue to Rule the World?" (keynote address, 60th Annual Meeting of the Rural Sociological Society, August 1997), 3.

11. Presbyterian Church (USA), "Affirming the Life of Rural Communities . . ." (report adopted by the 212th General Assembly, Long Beach, Calif., July 2000).

12. George M. Anderson, "Hungry in America," *America* (April 22, 2000): 18.

13. For a more complete understanding of this dynamic, see chap. 6 in Shannon Jung et al., *Rural Ministry: The Shape of the Renewal to Come* (Nashville: Abingdon, 1998); also Judith Bortner Heffernan, "Why the Crisis in Family Farms?" *Quaker Life* (March 2000), 12–13, 24. See also William Greider, "The Last Farm Crisis: The New Politics of Food," *The Nation* (November 20, 2000), 11–18.

14. Presbyterian Church (USA), "Affirming the Life of Rural Communities . . ." (see n. 11 above).

15. One of the best short summaries of the present state of United States farming is in the Presbyterian statement *We Are What We Eat* (Office of the General Assembly, 2002), 9–17. The entire resource can be ordered by contacting Diana Stephen 888/728-7228, ext. 5232 or dstephen@ctr.pcusa .org.

16. Elizabeth Becker, "Cattle Disease Poses Threat to Run Wild, U.S. Finds," *New York Times* (April 17, 2001), online edition.

17. Eva Jensen, executive director for Agricultural Missions, Church World Service and Witness, National Council of Churches (New York), in "Table Agenda: Interconnectedness of the Issues," speech at the Churches Center for Land and People, Sinsinawa, Wisc. (June 21, 2000), 5.

18. See Karen Lehman and Al Krebs, "Control of the World's Food Supply," in *The Case against the Global Economy, and for a Turn toward the Local*, ed. Jerry Mander and Edward Goldsmith (San Francisco: Sierra Club Books, 1996), 127.

19. Greider, "Last Farm Crisis," 16.

20. Ibid.

21. Ibid.

22. Ibid.

23. *International Herald Tribune* (May 21–22, 2001).

24. See Leslie Brenner, *American Appetite: The Coming of Age of a National Cuisine* (New York: HarperCollins, 1999).

25. Greg Winter, "Contaminated Foods Make Millions Ill Despite Advances," *New York Times* (March 24, 2001), online edition.

26. Ibid.

27. Malcolm Gladwell, "The Trouble with Fries," *The New Yorker* (March 5, 2001), 55.

28. Ibid., 53.

29. Eric Schlosser, *Fast Food Nation: The Dark Side of the All-American Meal* (Boston: Houghton Mifflin, 2001), 264.

30. Ibid., 242.

31. Ibid., chaps. 8 and 9.

32. Salt of the Earth, Social Justice News, December 2002, quoting a study by the Worldwatch Institute.

33. J. E. Young, "Aluminum's Real Tab," *World Watch* (March/April 1992), 26–33.

34. Brian Hallwell and Dani Niernberg, "Listen to This Wake-Up Call from Farm Animals," *International Herald Tribune* (March 15, 2001), 10.

35. Nessan, *Give Us This Day*, chap. 3.

36. The sequence of how the neglect of complicity develops into addiction is one area I hope a more qualified investigator will explore.

37. Nessan, *Give Us This Day*, chap. 4.

38. Ibid.

6. REDEEMING OUR LIVES

1. Judith Bortner Heffernan, "Why the Crisis in Family Farms?" *Quaker Life* (March 2000), 13.

2. Ibid., 24.

3. Ibid.

4. Ibid.

5. Ibid.

6. Malcolm Gladwell, "The Trouble with Fries," *New Yorker* (March 5, 2001), 57.

7. Quoted in ibid., 57.

8. See the entire article by Laura Fraser, "The Diet Trap," *Networker* (May/June 1997).

9. John Calvin, *Institutes of the Christian Religion,* ed. John T. McNeill, trans. Ford Lewis Battles, Library of Christian Classics (Philadelphia: Westminster, 1960 [orig. pub. 1559]), 1.13.1. The major way God accommodated us was through the incarnation itself, of course.

10. Ibid., 1.3.1

11. Howard L. Harrod, *The Animals Came Dancing: Native American Sacred Ecology and Animal Kinship* (Tucson: University of Arizona Press, 2000), xxiv.

12. The Reformed understanding of the *divinitatis sensum* makes a valuable point in terms of the question of human effort and initiative in realizing salvation. Ultimately all life, all human effort and initiative, has its source in God. God is the Creator and is also ongoing creativity, as Gordon Kaufman is fond of saying. Thus, to characterize God as especially taking initiative in the phase of awareness/acknowledgment is as false as suggesting—as we will—that human effort and initiative come more to the forefront in the phase of transformation. Human effort and desire for God come from God. God has enabled humankind to act, even against the divine. Thus, humankind is graced with seriousness, but has its being in God, even in rebellion. One of my favorite dicta of Jonathan Edwards is his statement that in salvation "God does it all, and we [human beings] do it all." This view no doubt derives from Edwards's view that all being emanates from Being-in-General.

13. Lisa Dahill, "A Woman's Secret Shame," *Daughters of Sarah* 19, no. 4 (fall 1993): 5.

14. Simone Weil, quoted in Jennifer Ruth Smith, "One Woman's Journey with Anorexia," *Daughters of Sarah* 19, no. 4 (fall 1993): 40.

15. Wendell Berry, "The Idea of a Local Economy," *Orion* (winter 2001), 28, 30. Berry is speaking specifically of our complicity "in the behavior of the corporation." The emphasis on being complicit in the actions of corporations is an important one for eaters to note.

16. I am uncomfortable speaking of the individual process of coming to redemption—the focus of this chapter—without noting the social nature of confession and transformation as well. They are always somewhat interrelated. Let me simply indicate that the next chapter focuses more on the communal aspects of redemption.

17. Mark Buchanan, "Go Fast and Live: Hunger as Spiritual Discipline," *Christian Century* 118, no. 7 (February 28, 2001), 16.

18. Mark Buchanan's article reminds us that consumption is killing us—it allows us to settle for the secondary rather than the primary beauty.

19. Garret Keizer, "A Time to Keep Kosher," *Christian Century* 117, no. 12 (April 19–26, 2000), 448. His article reminds us that fasting can consist of careful eating in several ways, not just denying all food.

20. Ibid., 449.

21. Terry Hershey, *Soul Gardening: Cultivating the Good Life* (Minneapolis: Augsburg, 2000), 11.

22. Ibid., 86, 104.

23. Joanne Harris, *Chocolat* (New York: Penguin, 2000), 51, 52.

7. A New Vision for the Church

1. Greg Critser, *Fat Land: How Americans Became the Fattest People in the World* (Boston: Houghton Mifflin, 2003).

2. David Leonhardt, "If Richer Isn't Happier, What Is?" *New York Times*, (May 19, 2001), online edition.

3. Monika Hellwig, *The Eucharist and the Hunger of the World*, 2nd ed. (Franklin, Wis.: Sheed & Ward, 1992), 32.

4. Ibid., 33.

5. Ibid., 53.

6. Karen Bloomquist, "Engaging Economic Globalization as a Communion," a report from the department for Theology and Studies, Lutheran World Federation, May 2001. Available from LWF, P.O. Box 2100, 150 route de Ferney, CH1211 Geneva 2, Switzerland.

7. Sallie McFague, *Life Abundant: Rethinking Theology and Ecology for a Planet in Peril* (Minneapolis: Fortress Press, 2001), 197.

8. Ibid., 198.

9. Ibid.

10. David Korten, *The Post-Corporate World: Life after Capitalism* (San Francisco: Berrett-Koehler; West Hartford, Conn.: Kumarian Press, 1999). See also Korten, *When Corporations Rule the World* (West Hartford, Conn.: Kumarian Press; San Francisco: Berrett-Koehler, 1995).

11. Korten, *Post-Corporate World*, 259, 263.

12. Ibid., 81.

13. This saying hung over Jung's office in Zurich and was carved on his tombstone.

14. John Dominic Crossan, *Jesus: A Revolutionary Biography* (San Francisco: HarperSanFrancisco, 1994), 73–74.

15. McFague, *Life Abundant*, 204.

16. Ibid.

17. For the ways we as individuals and the church as a corporate body can begin to implement some of these policies, see Presbyterian Church (USA), *We Are What We Eat* (Report approved by the 214th General Assembly, 2002), 17–33 (for marketing suggestions, resources, recommendations, and a Bible study). Available by calling 888-728-7228, ext. 5232, or contacting dstephen@ctr.pcusa.org.

Selected Bibliography

I. Food and Agriculture

Abelman, Michael, and Cynthia Wisehart. *On Good Land: The Autobiography of an Urban Farm*. San Francisco: Chronicle, 1998.

Berry, Wendell. *The Art of the Commonplace: The Agrarian Essays of Wendell Berry*. Edited by Norman Wirzba. Washington, D.C.: Counterpoint, 2002.

———. *Home Economics*. San Francisco: North Point, 1987.

———. *The Unsettling of America: Culture and Agriculture*. San Francisco: Sierra Club, 1977.

Biotechnology and Genetic Engineering. Toronto: Task Force on the Churches and Corporate Responsibility, Division of Mission in Canada, The United Church of Canada, 2000.

Boucher, Douglas. *The Paradox of Plenty: Hunger in a Bountiful World*. Oakland, Calif.: Food First, 1999.

Brenner, Leslie. *American Appetite: The Coming of Age of a National Cuisine*. New York: HarperCollins, 1999.

Commission on 21st Century Production Agriculture, *The Status of U.S. Agriculture* (Washington, D.C.: Commission on 21st Century Agriculture, 1998. To order: c/o Office of the Chief Economist, Room 112-A, J. L. Whitten Federal Building, 1400 Independence Ave. SW, Washington, D.C. 20250-3810; fax 202-690-4420.

Cuoto, Richard. *An American Challenge: A Report on Economic Trends and Social Issues in Appalachia*. Dubuque, Ia.: Kendall/Hunt, 1994.

Davidson, Osha Grey. *Broken Heartland: Rise of the Rural Ghetto*. New York: Doubleday, 1990. Revised 1996 by University of Iowa Press.

Gilbert, Charlene, and Quinn Eli. *Homecoming: The Story of African-American Farmers*. Boston: Beacon, 2000.

Heffernan, William, et al. *Consolidation in Food Retailing and Dairy: Implications for Farmers and Consumers in a Global Food System*. Columbia: University of Missouri, Department of Rural Sociology, 2001.

Jackson, Wes. *Becoming Native to This Place*. Lexington: University Press of Kentucky, 1994.

———. *New Roots for Agriculture*. San Francisco: Friends of the Earth; Salina, Kans.: Land Institute, 1986.

Jackson, Wes, and William Vitek. *Rooted in the Land: Essays on Community and Place*. New Haven: Yale University Press, 1996.

Lappé, Frances Moore. *Diet for a Small Planet*. New York: Ballantine, 1971.

Lappé, Frances Moore, and Joseph Collins. *World Hunger: Twelve Myths*. New York: Grove Weidenfeld, 1986.

Lappé, Frances Moore, and Anna Lappé. *Hope's Edge*. New York: Tarcher/Putnam, 2002.

Lind, Christopher. *Something's Wrong Somewhere: Globalization, Community, and the Moral Economy of the Farm Crisis*. Halifax, Nova Scotia: Fernwood, 1995.

Nabhan, Gary Paul. *Coming Home to Eat: The Pleasures and Politics of Local Foods*. New York: Norton, 2001.

Nestle, Marion. *Food Politics: How the Food Industry Influences Nutrition and Health*. Berkeley: University of California Press, 2002.

Presbyterian Church (USA). *We Are What We Eat*. Report approved by the 214th General Assembly, 2002. Available from Presbyterian Distribution Service, 1-800-524-2612, refer to PDS# 68-600-02-003.

Robbins, John. *Diet for a New America*. Walpole, N.H.: Stillpoint, 1987.

———. *The Food Revolution: How Your Diet Can Help Save Your Life and the World*. Berkeley, Calif.: Conari, 2001.

Ryan, John, and Alan Durning. *Stuff: The Secret Lives of Everyday Things*. Seattle, Wash.: Northwest Environment Watch, 1997.

Schlosser, Eric. *Fast Food Nation: The Dark Side of the All-American Meal*. Boston: Houghton Mifflin, 2001. Reprinted with new afterword 2002 by Perennial.

Shiva, Vandana. *Biopiracy: The Plunder of Nature and Knowledge*. Cambridge, Mass.: South End, 1997.

———. *Stolen Harvest: The Hijacking of the Global Food Supply*. Cambridge, Mass.: South End, 2000.

———. *The Violence of the Green Revolution*. London: Zed, 1992.

Sider, Ron. *Rich Christians in an Age of Hunger*. Dallas, Tex.: Word, 1990.

Strange, Marty. *Family Farming: A New Economic Vision*. Lincoln: University of Nebraska Press, 1988.

USDA National Commission on Small Farms. *A Time to Act.* Washington, D.C.: U.S. Department of Agriculture, January 1998. Available from the USDA, 1400 Independence Ave. SW, Washington, D.C. 20250.

II. CHRISTIAN ECOLOGICAL THEOLOGY

Austin, Richard Cartwright. *Hope for the Land: Nature in the Bible.* Atlanta: John Knox, 1988.

Berry, Thomas Mary. *The Dream of the Earth.* San Francisco: Sierra Club, 1988.

Bhagat, Shantilal P., ed. *God's Earth, Our Home.* A packet for congregational study and action on environmental and economic justice, available through Office of Environmental Justice, Presbyterian Church (USA), 100 Witherspoon Street, Room 3069, Louisville, KY 40202, 502-569-5809.

Boff, Leonardo. *Ecology and Liberation: A New Paradigm.* Maryknoll, N.Y.: Orbis, 1995.

Brueggemann, Walter. *The Land: Place as Gift, Promise, and Challenge in Biblical Faith.* Philadelphia: Fortress Press, 1997.

Delgado, Sharon. *Hope for the Earth—A Handbook for Christian Environmental Groups.* Service Department, General Board of Church and Society, United Methodist Church, 100 Maryland Ave. NE, Washington, D.C. 20002, 1-800-967-0880.

DeWitt, Calvin. *Earthwise: A Biblical Response to Environmental Issues.* Grand Rapids: Christian Reformed Church, 1994.

Eco-Justice Working Group, *Faith-Based Environmental Justice Resources for Youth and Children.* New York: National Council of Churches of Christ in the USA, 1993. To order: Environmental Justice Resources, NCC, P.O. Box 968, Elkhart, IN 46515, 1-800-762-0968 or 212-264-3102.

Hellwig, Monika. *The Eucharist and the Hunger of the World.* Franklin, Wisc.: Sheed & Ward, 1992.

Hessel, Dieter, ed. *After Nature's Revolt: Eco-Justice and Theology.* Minneapolis: Augsburg Fortress Press, 1992.

Jung, Shannon. *We Are Home: A Spirituality of the Environment.* Mahwah, N.J.: Paulist, 1993.

McFague, Sallie. *The Body of God: An Ecological Theology.* Minneapolis: Fortress Press, 1993.

———. *Life Abundant: Rethinking Theology and Ecology for a Planet in Peril.* Minneapolis: Fortress Press, 2001.

———. *Models of God: Theology for an Ecological, Nuclear Age.* Philadelphia: Fortress Press, 1987.

———. *Super, Natural Christians: How We Should Love Nature.* Minneapolis: Fortress Press, 1997.

Presbyterian Church (USA). *Restoring Creation for Ecology and Justice.* Report adopted by the 202nd General Assembly, 1990. Available from Presbyterian Distribution Services, 1-800-524-2612, refer to PDS #OGA-90-002.

Radford Ruether, Rosemary. *Gaia and God: An Ecofeminist Thelogy of Earth Healing.* San Francisco: HarperSanFrancisco, 1992.

———. *Women Healing Earth: Third World Women on Ecology, Feminism and Religion.* Maryknoll, N.Y.: Orbis, 1996.

Rasmussen, Larry. *Earth Community, Earth Ethics.* Maryknoll, N.Y.: Orbis, 1996.

Roberts, Elizabeth, and Elias Amidon. *Earth Prayers from Around the World.* New York: HarperCollins, 1991.

Santmire, H. Paul. *The Travail of Nature: The Ambiguous Ecological Promise of Christian Theology.* Philadelphia: Fortress Press, 1985.

Schut, Michael, ed. *Food & Faith: Justice, Joy, and Daily Bread.* Denver, Colo.: Living the Good News, 2002. A compendium of articles from Earth Ministry.

III. GLOBAL ECONOMICS AND THE GLOBAL FOOD SUPPLY SYSTEM

Beckmann, David, and Arthur Simon. *Grace at the Table: Ending Hunger in God's World.* New York: Paulist, 1999.

Cobb, Clifford, Ted Halsted, and Jonathan Rowe. "If the GDP Is Up, Why Is America Down?" *Atlantic Monthly,* October 1995.

Cobb, John B. Jr. *Sustainability: Economics, Ecology, and Justice.* Maryknoll, N.Y.: Orbis, 1995.

Daly, Herman, and John B. Cobb Jr. *For the Common Good: Redirecting the Economy toward Community, the Environment, and a Sustainable Future.* Boston: Beacon, 1989.

Dawn, Marva. *Unfettered Hope: A Call to Faithful Living in an Affluent Society.* Louisville: Westminster John Knox, 2003.

Durning, Alan. *How Much Is Enough? The Consumer Society and the Future of the Earth.* New York: Norton, 1992.

Foster, Richard. *The Freedom of Simplicity.* San Francisco: Harper & Row, 1981.

Hawken, Paul. *The Ecology of Commerce: Doing Good Business.* New York: HarperCollins, 1993.

Hawken, Paul, Amory Lovins, and L. Hunter Lovins. *Natural Capitalism: Creating the Next Industrial Revolution.* Boston: Little, Brown, 1999.

Korten, David. *The Post-Corporate World: Life after Capitalism.* West Hartford, Conn.: Kumarian and San Francisco: Berrett-Koehler, 1999.

———. *When Corporations Rule the World.* West Hartford, Conn.: Kumarian and San Francisco: Berrett-Koehler, 1995.

Mander, Jerry, and Edward Goldsmith, eds. *The Case against the Global Economy: And for a Turn toward the Local.* San Francisco: Sierra Club, 1996.

Meadows, Donella H. *Beyond the Limits: Confronting Global Collapse, Envisioning a Sustainable Future.* Mills, Vt.: Chelsea Green, 1992.

Nessan, Craig L. *Give Us This Day: A Lutheran Response to World Hunger.* Minneapolis: Fortress Press, 2003.

Schumacher, E. F. *Small Is Beautiful: Economics as If People Mattered.* New York: Harper & Row, 1973.

Schut, Michael, ed. *Simpler Living, Compassionate Life: A Christian Perspective.* Denver, Colo.: Living the Good News, 1999.

Simon, Arthur. *How Much Is Enough? Hungering for God in an Affluent Culture.* Grand Rapids: Baker, 2003.

IV. FOOD PRACTICES AND EATING DISORDERS

Altman, Donald. *Art of the Inner Meal: Eating as a Spiritual Path.* San Francisco: Harper, 1999.

Barth, Marcus. *Rediscovering the Lord's Supper: Communion with Israel, with Christ, and among the Guests.* Atlanta: John Knox, 1987.

Brumberg, Joan Jacobs. *The Body Project: An Intimate History of American Girls.* New York: Random House, 1997.

Bullitt-Jonas, Margaret. *Holy Hunger: A Memoir of Desire.* New York: Alfred A. Knopf, 1999.

Capron, Robert F. *The Supper of the Lamb.* New York: Harcourt Brace, 1967.

Childs, James M. Jr. *Greed: Economics and Ethics in Conflict.* Minneapolis: Fortress Press, 2000.

Critser, Eric. *Fat Land: How Americans Became the Fattest People in the World.* Boston: Houghton Mifflin, 2003.

Hershey, Terry. *Soul Gardening: Cultivating the Good Life.* Minneapolis: Augsburg, 2000.

Juengst, Sara Covin. *Breaking Bread: The Spiritual Significance of Food.* Louisville: Westminster John Knox, 1992.

Kass, Leon. *The Hungry Soul: Eating and the Perfecting of Our Nature.* Chicago: University of Chicago Press, 1994. Reprinted 1999.

Koenig, John. *The Feast of the World's Redemption: Eucharistic Origins and Christian Mission.* Harrisburg, Pa.: Trinity Press International, 2000.

Lelwica, Michelle. *Starving for Salvation: The Spiritual Dimensions of Eating Problems among American Girls and Women.* New York: Oxford University Press, 1999.

Nelson, James B. *Embodiment: An Approach to Sexuality and Christian Theology.* Minneapolis: Augsburg, 1978.

Pipher, Mary. *Reviving Ophelia: Saving the Selves of Adolescent Girls.* New York: Ballantine, 1995.

Pope, Harrison Jr., Katharine A. Phillips, and Roberto Olivardia. *The Adonis Complex: The Secret Crisis of Male Body Obsession.* New York: Free Press, 2000.

Scarry, Elaine. *The Body in Pain: The Making and Unmaking of the World.* New York: Oxford University Press, 1985.

Schlosser, Eric. *Fast Food Nation: The Dark Side of the All-American Meal.* Boston: Houghton Mifflin, 2001. Reprinted with new afterword 2002 by Perennial.

Thompson, Marjorie J. *Soul Feast: An Invitation to the Christian Spiritual Life.* Foreword by Henri J. M. Nouwen. Louisville, Ky.: Westminster John Knox, 1995.

Volf, Miroslav, and Dorothy Bass, eds. *Practicing Theology: Beliefs and Practices in the Christian Life.* Grand Rapids: Eerdmans, 2001.

Webb, Stephen. *Good Eating.* Waco, Tex.: Brazos, 2001.

Appendix 1: Video Resources

Affluenza: The Cost of High Living. An excellent video, produced by John DeGraaf and public TV station KCTS in Seattle, that highlights environmental, social, community, and spiritual costs of consumption. A significant portion of *Affluenza* focuses on a Christian response to overconsumerism. Sixty minutes with a guide for group discussion. Call 800-937-5387.

Beyond Organic: The Vision of Fairview Gardens. Produced by John DeGraaf (producer of *Affluenza*), this inspiring video tells the story of Fairview Gardens and its struggle to survive in the face of rapid suburban development. It draws a sharp contrast between community supported agriculture and conventional chemical farming. Thirty-three minutes. Bullfrog Films, P.O. Box 149, Oley, PA 19547, 800-543-3764, bullfrogfilms.com.

Delafield. Produced by Mark Brodin (contact No Boy At All, LLC, email: Brodin@USinternet.com.) In 1998 the congregation of Delafield in southwestern Minnesota celebrated their 125th year. Four months later, faced with the harsh realities of a changing rural life, the community disbanded the congregation and gave away their beloved church building. Old-timers talk about a lifetime spent on the land. They convey a love of farming and a passion for their calling, articulating how difficult it is to leave behind this vanishing way of life.

The Farmer's Wife. Co-produced by Donald Sutherland and Frontline, in association with the Independent Television Service and aired on Public Television Stations nationwide in 1998. Three tapes, $49.98. This video documents three years in the life of Juanita and Darrell Buschkoetter, a young farm couple living in Nebraska. It is a powerful presentation of the economic and emotional struggles experienced by their farm as a result of economic depression.

From this Valley . . . On Defending the Family Farm, produced by the Division of Church and Society, National Council of Churches, 1986. A historical overview of agriculture is provided in this video, highlighting the mechanical, chemical, and biotechnical revolutions. It continues by discussing why churches need to defend the mid-size family farm. This video provides excellent orientation to the issues and can serve as a "discussion starter." Eighteen minutes.

The Global Banquet: Politics of Food, produced by Maryknoll World Productions, P.O. Box 308, Maryknoll, NY 10545-0308, 800-227-8523, www.maryknollworld.org. Total of fifty minutes divided into two twenty-five-minute segments. "This timely, provocative video explores the politics of global food security—a security threatened by the policies and practices of giant international food producers, trade and financial institutions, as well as governments here and abroad" (quote from the discussion/study guide). Discussion and study guide available.

Hot Potatoes. Explores the dangers of potato blight and the chemicals used to control it. More than 150 years after Ireland's potato famine, late blight is still an immense global threat. Potatoes have gradually become one of the world's three most important sources of nutrition, especially in developing nations. But the failure to heed the warnings of an exceptional scientist in the 1950s is having dire consequences at the beginning of the twenty-first century. Fifty-seven minutes. Bullfrog Films, P.O. Box 149, Oley, PA 19547, 800-543-3764, www.bullfrogfilms.com.

Reclaiming Our Rural Heritage: A Time to Act. A video produced by and available from Catholic Charities, Diocese of Sioux City, Iowa; att: Marilyn Murphy, Box 1342, Sioux City, IA 51102, 712-255-4346, fax 712-255-5328. Cost $10, includes shipping and handling. Allow two weeks for delivery. Video describing rural issues—especially the current farm crisis—and why the church should be involved. Fifty-five minutes.

Stewards of Creation, Stewards of Hope. A video produced by the North Dakota Conference of Churches. For more information about the video or to obtain a copy, contact: North Dakota Conference of Churches, 227 West Broadway, Suite 2, Bismarck, ND 58501, 701-255-0604. The focus of this video is on stewardship of creation in the context of the late 1990s. Thirty-five minutes.

Who's Counting? Marilyn Waring on Sex, Lies, and Global Economics. Waring challenges the myths of economics and our tacit compliance with political agendas that masquerade as objective economic policy. Bullfrog Films, P.O.

Box 149, Oley, PA 19547, 800-543-3764, www.bullfrogfilms.com. Ninety-four minutes.

The World Trade Organization: The Whole World in Whose Hands? A video produced by the Women's Division, General Board of Global Ministries, The United Methodist Church. For more information call 1-800-305-9857. This video produces case studies, explanations, and questions regarding the World Trade Organization. Twenty minutes.

Zenith. Produced by Prairie Fire Films, www.zeniththemovie.com. The documentary tells the story of a tiny town dying on the plains of Kansas that finds transformation and redemption by producing and performing in what is known as the Great Plains Passion Play.

Appendix 2: Educational Resources

1. Presbyterian Church (USA)

www.pcusa.org
National Ministries Division:
    Advisory Committee on Social Witness Policy
    Mission Responsibility through Investment
    New Immigrant Ministries in the USA
    Presbyterian Disaster Assistance
    Presbyterian Health, Education, and Welfare Association
    Presbyterian Hunger Program
    Rural Ministry Office
    Self-Development of People
    Washington Office
    Women's Ministries
    Worldwide Ministries Division:

2. Evangelical Lutheran Church in America
www.elca.org

3. Educational links

www.newdream.org
    Center for a New American Dream. 6930 Carroll Ave., Suite 900, Takoma Park, MD 20912. Connecting food choices with greater equity; kid-friendly and educational.

www.ruralministry.com
    Center for Theology and Land, University of Dubuque and Wartburg Seminaries, Dubuque, Iowa. Theological and congregational resources; conferences; links to other sites. Syllabus on theology of eating. 2000 University Ave., Dubuque, IA 52001, 563-589-3117.

www.earthsave.org
EarthSave. Chapters throughout the country; excellent food-specific publications, 800-362-3648.

www.foodfirst.org
Food First. Think tank and education-action center. 398 60th Street, Oakland, CA 94618, 510-654-4400.

www.heifer.org
Heifer Project International. Global outreach to farmers and communities. Education and action for all ages. P.O. Box 8058, Little Rock, AR 72203, 800-422-0474.

www.ifg.org
International Forum on Globalization. International and agricultural think tank.

www.landstewardshipproject.org
Land Stewardship Project. Educational and activist ecological organization.

www.rsse.tamu.edu
Rural Social Science Education. Fargo, ND.

4. CHURCH-RELATED LINKS

www.bread.org
Bread for the World. Washington, D.C. Nationwide organization guiding citizens to lobby legislators about world hunger issues.

www.cam-web.org
Coalition for Appalachian Ministries. Townsend, TN.

www.earthministry.org
Earth Ministry. An ecumenical, Christian, environmental, eco-justice oriented nonprofit organization, based in Seattle, WA.

www.ncrlc.org
National Catholic Rural Life Conference. Advocacy-oriented, educational, faith-grounded organization with local reps nationwide. Food campaign. 4625 Beaver Ave., Des Moines, IA 50310, 515-270-2634.

www.nfwm.org
National Farm Worker Ministry. National office in St. Louis, MO 63130, 314-726-6470.

www.webofcreation.org

Web of Creation. Transforming faith-based communities for a sustainable and just world.

5. COMMUNITY ORGANIZATION LINKS

www.farmland.org

American Farmland Trust. Conservation and preservation legal society, Washington, D.C.

www.coc.org

Center of Concern. Food Security Project, Washington, D.C.

www.newcomm.org

Center for New Community, Oak Park, Ill. Faith-based organizing initiatives to revitalize rural congregations and communities for genuine social, economic, and political democracy.

www.cfra.org

Center for Rural Affairs. Walthill, Neb.

www.citizens.org

Citizens for Health. Empowers citizens to make informed health choices.

www.caff.org

Community Alliance with Family Farmers. Political and educational campaigns. Publishes the *National Organic Directory.*

www.foodsecurity.org

Community Food Security Coalition.

www.coopamerica.org

Co-op America. Links consumers with eco-responsible businesses. A nationwide "green" marketplace. *National Green Pages.* 1612 K St. NW, Suite 600, Washington, D.C. 20006, 800-584-7336.

Dakota Rural Action

Dakota Rural Action. Brookings, SD. Email: action@dakotarural.org

www.federationsoutherncoop.com

Federation of Southern Cooperatives. Focus on African American farmers, East Point, Ga.

www.foodandwater.org

Food and Water. Campaigns against toxic foods.

www.foodcircles.missouri.edu

Food Circles Networking Project. Oriented to food security and toward local food buying. Great links.

www.iatp.org

Institute for Agriculture & Trade Policy.

www.sustainableagriculture.net

National Campaign for Sustainable Agriculture. Pine Bush, N.Y.

www.nffc.net

National Family Farm Coalition. Washington, D.C.

www.nfu.org

National Farmers Union. Denver, Colo.

www.navs-online.org

North American Vegetarian Society. Dolgeville, N.Y.

www.panna.igc.org

Pesticide Action Network. Works to replace harmful pesticides with safer alternatives.

www.ruralco.org

Rural Coalition. A multicultural, grassroots organization with advocacy, educational, and marketing outreach, based in Washington, D.C.

www.seedsavers.com.

Seed Savers Exchange. Preserves heirloom breeds throughout the world. 3076 North Winn Rd., Decorah, IA 52101, 563-382-5590.

www.slowfood.com

Slow Food USA. Gastronomic movement featuring local cuisines. Worldwide chapters. P.O. Box 1737, New York, NY 10021.

www.sare.org

Sustainable Agriculture Research and Education. Education and links.

www.webofcreation.org

Web of Creation. Seeks to provide faith-based communities with "sustainable diet" information and related resources.

www.worc.org

Western Organization of Resource Councils. Billings, Mont.

6. GOVERNMENT LINKS

www.usda.gov
Department of Agriculture.

www.biodynamics.com.
Biodynamic Farming and Gardening Association. Contact them for most updated list of CSAs in your area. 800-516-7797.

www.nal.usda.gov/afsic/csa
Information on CSA movement. Resources for Community Supported Agriculture (CSA) and Farmers Markets.

www.ams.usda.gov/farmersmarkets/
A national listing of farmers markets.

www.localharvest.org
Local Harvest. Most comprehensive list of all CSAs, farmers markets, u-pick locations, and related information.

7. COFFEE LINKS

www.equalexchange.org
Equal Exchange. Supports small farmers globally. 251 Revere St., Canton, MA 02021, 781-830-0303. Coffee to your door in four days.

www.orcacoffee.org Organic Coffee Association.

www.songbird.org
The Songbird Foundation. Makes sustainable coffee choices to preserve migratory songbirds and their habitats.

www.transfairusa.org
TransFair USA. 1611 Telegraph Ave., Suite 900, Oakland, CA 94612, 520-663-5260. Promotes fair trade products all over the world.

8. ANIMAL TREATMENT LINKS

www.crle.org
Center for Respect of Life and Environment. Educational promoter of humane and sustainable future for animals and humans. 2100 L St. NW, Washington, D.C. 20037, 202-778-6133.

www.farmusa.org
Farm Animal Reform Movement. Promotes vegetarianism and well-being of farm animals. P.O. Box 30654, Bethseda, MD 20824, 888-FARM-USA.

www.fund.org

The Fund for Animals. Protects wildlife and domestic animals. 200 West 57th St., Suite 705, New York, NY 10019, 888-405-FUND.

www.factoryfarm.org

GRACE Factory Farm Project. Helps oppose the spread of factory farms; addresses impact of factory farming. 145 Spruce St., Lititz, PA 17543, 717-627-0410.

www.hfa.org

Humane Farming Association. Works to stop animal abuse, conducts education, advocacy, legislation. P.O. Box 3577, San Rafael, CA 94912, 415-485-1495.

Index